D0126244

NOSTRADAMUS PREDICTS THE END OF THE WORLD

RENE NOORBERGEN

formerly titled
INVITATION TO A HOLOCAUST

Research by Joey Jochmans

PINNACLE BOOKS   NEW YORK

NOSTRADAMUS PREDICTS THE END OF THE WORLD

Pinnacle Books edition, published by arrangement with St. Martin's Press. Formerly titled *Invitation to a Holocaust*

First printing / July 1982

ISBN: 0-523-42366-7

Printed in the United States of America

PINNACLE BOOKS, INC.
1430 Broadway
New York, New York 10018

9   8   7   6   5

NOSTRADAMUS
FORECASTS W.W.III

Sometime before 1995, Russia and the United States will ally themselves against China, the Middle East, and Latin America in the most destructive and terrifying war the world has ever experienced. In what may well become the Last Great War, conducted by conventional and nuclear weaponry as well as by biological warfare, no continent will escape devastation.

This theory was originally propounded in verse form by Michel de Nostredame, better known as Nostradamus, in 1555 in a book entitled *Les Vrayes Centuries*—the true centuries. Since its publication, nearly two-thirds of Nostradamus's prophecies have been fulfilled, and most of the remaining predictions are, according to the dates and astrological configurations they contain, due to occur within the next two decades.

The legendary psychic foresaw—as far back as the fourteenth century—that friendly relations would open up between Russia and the United States who would then join forces with Western Europe. According to Nostradamus's scenario, the peoples of the Far East and the Middle East will retaliate and prepare for armed conflict supported by the nuclear and bacteriological arsenal of Red China. Israel will be one of the first victims of the Arab allies who will then press into Europe, the scene of much of the fighting. China will surprise the West with nuclear attacks and release bacteriological bombs over Alaska. And when the Western allies begin to take a nuclear offensive, the Easterners will already have moved into Latin America.

By the use of astrology and the application of his remarkable intuitive powers not unlike present-day psychics, Nostradamus not only specified the dimensions of what may well become *the* Holocaust of all time, but listed names of generals, rivers, mountains, and areas which will be involved.

In *Invitation to a Holocaust*, Rene Noorbergen interprets in the light of current affairs and modern technological capabilities the prophetic verses of the great visionary who has remained a popular figure into our own century.

About The Author:

Former war correspondent Rene Noorbergen has written eleven books including *Jeanne Dixon: My Life and Prophecies* (1969).

Contents

CHAPTER 6: THE LAST RESISTANCE—THE FALL OF EUROPE

CHAPTER 7: TURNING POINT—THE USA AND RUSSIA TAKE THE OFFENSIVE

CHAPTER 8: LIBERATION

List of Maps

Introduction

Things are never quite as simple as often they seem to be, and Joseph Goebbels, Minister of Propaganda for the wartime German cabinet, found that out the hard way. At least things didn't work out as Goebbels thought they would.

It was during the fall of the year preceding the unexpected German blitz-attack on the lowland countries of Holland and Belgium, that he had a quiet fireside chat with the Führer and brought him up to date with the latest evaluations of the compiled works of a French fortune-teller whose prophecies, he felt, had not only predicted Hitler's great rise to power, but had foretold the outcome as well—way back in the 1500s!

We don't know the extent of the Führer's enthusiasm for the strange-sounding prophecies, but we do know the results. It was only months later—in 1940 to be exact—that the German *Luftwaffe* dropped millions of "Nostradamian leaflets" on the unsuspecting lowland countries, telling those who found them that resistance to Hitler's advancing armies would be useless.

"His victory," they claimed "was prophesied centuries ago by a French seer named Nostradamus."

Did anyone take them seriously?

I am sure we will never know, but just to avoid the slim chance that someone might, British Intelligence followed it up with a drop of their own by the Royal Air Force, using fabricated Nostradamian prophecies that indicated just the opposite.

No one apparently worried about Nostradamus's copyright or his integrity, giving credence to the old saying that "all is fair in love and war."

By now, both the leaflets and the outcome of World War II are part of history, but although the yellowing leaflets are gathering dust on the shelves of the archives, the enigma of Nostradamus lives on, and undoubtedly will for many years to come.

Nostradamus is an enigma—there's no doubt about that. But he is more, much more, than that. Every researcher who has scrutinized his legacy of four-line poetic predictions usually becomes more bewildered with each passing line, for Nostradamus clearly had the ability to see beyond the veil of time. Although he died more than 400 years ago, his prophetic judgment and his supernatural grasp of developing history placed him first among equals; a super psychic among the clairvoyants of the ages.

Michel de Nostredame was born in 1503 in St. Rémy de Provence, in France, and was brought up as a Catholic although born in a Jewish household. Brilliant, witty, and inquisitive, he explored natural science, astronomy, philosophy and anatomy—the latter fascinated him so much that he enrolled at the University of Montpellier and graduated in 1529 as a doctor in medicine. He soon became well known throughout France because of his success in treating victims of the plague and the number of his other patients who survived! This was undoubtedly due to his blunt refusal to bleed his patients; a remedy widely used in his day but one which cost many lives.

There are many theories as to exactly how he received his vast foreknowledge of history, yet Nostradamus himself never tried to hide the techniques he used.

Astrology was at a peak in his time, and when he published his first collection of predictive poetry known as *Les Vrayes Centuries*—The True Centuries—in 1555, it was generally understood that he received his revelations solely from his observations of the heavens, in much the same way the old Assyrian and Babylonian astrologers practiced their predictive "science."

He never denied that this was indeed one of the methods of divination used by him, but he did not rule out all the other practices. We do know that he received many of his visions by gazing into the flat undisturbed surface of a bowl of water that had been placed on a brass tripod, in much the same way as a gypsy fortune-teller stares into her crystal ball. Whether the majority of his visions came to him in these ways or from a psychic inspiration, necromancy, tarot cards or a refined form of witchcraft, we will probably never learn. We might conclude, however, that his hidden source of knowledge knew much of the course history would take, and possibly had the power to control or at least influence some of the major future historical developments. But *what* in fact it was, or *who* really was behind it, Nostradamus never revealed, and the chances are that he was indeed totally ignorant of the identity of the mysterious power that controlled the phenomena which showed him the course of the future.

In some ways, he had intuitive powers not at all unlike some of today's leading psychics. It has been reported that one day, when he was still a young man and traveling in Italy, he fell on his knees before a passing monk named Felice Peretti. Overcome with emotion, and to the surprise and astonishment of the onlookers, Nostradamus blurted out, "I kneel before His Holiness." Later on in that same century, in 1585, the monk, now seasoned and much older, became Pope Sixtus V.

Nostradamus played a most dangerous game, and he knew it. His day was not only known for its superstition and belief in astrology, but it was also the celebrated Age of the Inquisition when millions were burned at the stake or died screaming on the rack, simply because they had been accused of heresy or witchcraft; and everything that could not be explained by a gullible priest *had* to be of a dark supernatural origin.

To avoid accusations of this sort, Nostradamus confused the dating and ranking of his predictions purposely, and wrote them in a truly bewildering mixture of symbols, Old French, anagrams, Latin and other literary devices, so as to be able to fool the investigators of the Inquisition should they ever come knocking at his door.

THE END OF THE WORLD

As far as is known, Nostradamus did not leave a "key" to his predictions with anyone. If he did, it has certainly been lost in the dust of the centuries. The need of having to interpret his predictions without the help of such an aid has led to some curious and widely varied versions of his quatrains. Yet many of them are so close to fact that his reputation as Europe's greatest psychic continues undiminished.

Although his first book of predictive verse—100 verses per book—was published in 1555, he began making prophecies as far back as 1547. Uttering some predictions that "hit home," he attracted the attention of Catherine de Medici who invited him to her palace, whereafter Charles IX appointed him physician-in-ordinary. However, Nostradamus's fame as a doctor faded when he failed to cure his own family of the plague but his reputation as a prophet grew to extraordinary dimensions.

Seeing the future and writing his visions down in quatrains, Nostradamus set out to compose 1,000 four-line verses, each possessing a specific prophecy on some future events locked within its symbolic words.

The "enigma of the centuries"—the man Nostradamus—has never been out of vogue, and during the past four hundred years, an army of commentators and interpreters has devoted at least a hundred learned volumes to deciphering and decoding the Nostradamian puzzles. Interpretations often differ because the verses might have been taken out of context but a logical account or responsible sequential story can be reached only if the seer's problem of having to work around the Inquisition is kept in mind, and sufficient time and energy are given to piecing the various predictions that deal with a certain event together, and to deciphering his symbolic language. No matter which method is used, however, even some of his individual predictions appear to have been fulfilled to an accuracy of somewhere between eighty-six and ninety-one per cent; the exact percentage depending on the bias of the interpreter.

Of all the predictions that can be found interwoven in the collection of Nostradamus's quatrains, those dealing with the last major armed conflict that will be fought on this tired old globe are truly frightening in every way. Not only does he specify the dimensions of what may well become the Last Great War, *the* Holocaust of all times, but he also lists names of generals, place names, rivers, mountains and areas which, because of our knowledge of geography and current affairs, are so obviously accurate that we can almost "see" the menacing hand of Mars hang over the remains of our already dying Western civilization.

What you are about to read are the two hundred and sixty-five prophetic quatrains of Nostradamus that describe a world-wide holocaust; a war which has yet to be fought. The conflict, according to the seer, will involve not only the United States and Russia, China, the Middle East and Latin America but many other areas. In fact the entire world will be involved, with nuclear bombs, bacteriological weapons and gas killing off the population in country after country. The destruction will be more devastating than anything ever experienced before by this world.

THE END OF THE WORLD

The time for this global clash between East and West has been set by Nostradamus at somewhere between the 1980s and 1995—this, based on astrological configurations.

It is scheduled to happen somewhere in our lifetime!
Are we ready for it?

Nostradamus's scenario for World War III, the Holocaust that will swamp all memories of all previous wars because of its ultimate horror, will start quietly while peace is prevailing throughout the world. It will be the change in Russia from Communism to a more tolerable form of government that will be the catalyst. Nostradamus predicts that this change in Russia will open the way for friendship between the United States and Russia, nations he calls the "two brothers of the Far North who will share communication across the Arctic Ocean."

A condition that looks like a blessing, will turn out to be a curse, for the developing friendship of the two super-nations will disturb the balance of power in the world, and shortly thereafter, when they combine their might with that of Western Europe, the peoples of the Far East and the Middle East will retaliate and get ready for an armed conflict supported by the nuclear and bacteriological/chemical arsenal of Red China.

One very surprising feature revealed in Nostradamus's prophecies is that, while there are numerous references to the extensive use of nuclear and bacteriological weapons, the two opposing sides in the conflict will also be actively engaged in invasions and counter-invasions involving conventional methods of warfare; including the movement of troops by air, land and sea.

It has often been thought that the next Great War will start with the pressing of buttons by soldiers hidden in deep underground caverns, and that it will end a matter of hours later with atomic destruction of the entire Western and Eastern civilizations. But military tacticians no longer agree with this pessimistic picture. Of all the possibilities of how a future war will be fought, the odds lean heavily in favor of a campaign in which one power will attempt to gain a decisive advantage over its enemy without risking utter destruction through retaliation. The experts foresee that a limited nuclear exchange will probably introduce the next war, but that it will be followed by conventional warfare, supplemented by nuclear field weapons only when they are deemed to be absolutely necessary.

This strategy, which is now generally accepted, agrees perfectly with Nostradamus's predictions.

Although Nostradamus has done a remarkable job of hiding the sequence of his forecast for World War III between less important predictions throughout his quatrains, painstaking research and literary detective work have nevertheless made it possible to identify those verses that deal with the Holocaust and, one can feel Nostradamus's mounting frustration and anguish, in reading his revelations.

Being French, the seer naturally saw the war from his European point of view, and he described the future of the warring powers of East and West in terms of how they were to affect the future of

THE END OF THE WORLD

Europe, as well as that of the United States *and* the Church of Rome.

That he foresees the major battles of World War III taking place in Europe may seem rather fortunate for the rest of the world, but the conflict will be so immense and so far-reaching, that although much of the killing and bloodshed will be on European soil, the other parts of the globe will not be able to escape the horrors of the holocaust. We have to admit, however, that in a conflict between the USA and Russia on one side and China, the Far East and the Middle East on the other side, Europe will undoubtedly be the most logical battleground for conventional warfare. The only hope for ultimate victory for China and her Far Eastern allies lies in completely encircling and isolating the two superpowers from each other and from the rest of the world. Europe is the major form of communications between them, and the conquest and destruction of Europe will therefore have to be a vital part of the Eastern strategy.

Close scrutiny of Nostradamus's predictions dealing with the New War shows us that they can be divided into nine specific parts; each one describing a particular phase of an especially dirty war.

It appears that Israel will be one of the first victims of the Arabs' plan for conquest; conquest of not just the Middle East but all of Europe as well. With the conflict mounting in Turkey, the defeat of the Greeks and the breakdown of peace negotiations in Geneva, the stage is being set for the second stage of the war when China hits the West with surprise nuclear attacks and releases her frightening bacteriological bombs over Alaska so that the diseases drift on the currents to the countries of the Western Alliance. This will be followed by a Chinese invasion of southern Russia.

Not to be outdone by the Far Eastern powers, the Arabs carry out a battle plan of their own by moving westward and attacking nations in "their" sphere of influence. Rome will soon be destroyed, civil war will break out in Italy, and France will feel forced to enter the spreading conflict, for by now enemy forces appear to be heading for France's borders.

When the third phase of the war begins, the French will be in the middle of a counter-offensive in Italy but, while they regroup after having been defeated, and England is becoming the victim of a flood that will devastate the country, the situation in Italy worsens, and the Pope will be forced to flee to a new land. These events happen almost simultaneously with the capture of Prince Albert of Monaco, and the dropping of atom bombs on Venice.

During the fourth phase we encounter the total destruction of Monaco and Chinese attacks on France; Chinese-Arab assaults on Spain, and extensive bombing of all of Europe. The fall of Switzerland and the last stand of the Allies near the Belgian city of Bruges can be considered typical of the long series of defeats that will plague the Allies throughout the first phases of the war.

It will not be until the seventh phase that the United States and Russia will finally go over to the offensive although up to that time the Easterners will already have moved into Latin America. Although Nostradamus does not predict exactly when the war in the Far East will come to an end, he does state that it will happen when the superpowers begin to use germ weapons on the Chinese and attack them in their home territory.

With the Allies now being able to concentrate all their manpower and firepower in the European theater, the liberation of Europe is only a matter of time. Submarine assault forces, germ and nuclear weapons and massive naval battles off the west coast of Spain will all play their role in the liberation of the European Allies and the return of the Pope to his demolished throne in a Vatican that exists only in memory.

In the light of international developments, it is extremely interesting that Nostradamus—as far back as the 1500s—gives the Middle Eastern nations a major fighting role in the war. This might seem somewhat implausible in the light of Israel's repeated military victories over her Arab neighbors in recent years, but while the Middle Eastern nations may not appear to be strong enough now, the next five years will undoubtedly witness a radical change. Already they are wielding tremendous economic power because of their oil reserves. The Russian influence in the region has been declining for a number of years, and the USA's insistence on support for Israel is rapidly undermining her influence in that part of the world. By exchanging their American and the Russian "benefactors" for Peking, the Arabs may find an ally who will have no qualms about supplying them with nuclear bombs as well as bacteriological/chemical and other more-conventional weapons. Once their arsenal has been rebuilt along those lines, they will strike west;

China will strike south and World War III will be upon us.

Here then is Nostradamus's forecast of The Holocaust.

Chapter 1

PRELUDE TO WAR

Q1. A Prophecy of the Present

Les fléaux passés diminue le monde,
Longtemps la paix terres inhabitées;
Sûr marchera par ciel, terre, mer et onde,
Puis de nouveau les guerres suscitées. (I, 63)

The scourges passed, and the world shrinks,
There will be peace for a long time and lands
    will decrease in population.
One will travel safely by air, land, and through
    sea and wave,
But then war will be stirred up again!

There is little need to interpret the translation of
this Nostradamus quatrain, for he clearly states
that our relatively peaceful age will be distinguished
by advances in communication, causing a "shrink-
ing of the world"; he refers to the population
explosion and the commercial travel in the air, on

land and sea and below the sea. His statement is definite—but so is his prediction that war will follow.

Q2–Q4. A Revolutionary Change in Russia

La loi Moricque on verra défaillir:
Après une autre beaucoup plus seductive:
Boristhenes premier viendra faillir:
Par dons et langue une plus attractive. (III,95)

Ès lieux et temps chair au poisson donnera lieu,
La loi commune sera faite au contraire:
Vieux tiendra fort puis ôtée du milieu,
La Panta Chiona Philon mis fort arriere. (IV,32)

De gent esclave, chansons, chants et requêtes,
Captifs par Princes et Seigneurs aux prisons:
À l'avenir par idiots sans têtes,
Seront reçus par divines oraisons. (I,14)

The Law of Thomas More (communism) will decline,
Acceptance of another philosophy will be more appealing.
The River Dnieper [west Russia] will give way first
Given goods by another nation more attractive.

At the places and times when there is a religious abstinence [Easter],
The Communist law will be opposed

14

The old leaders will strongly support it but
    they will be removed from power,
"Loving of Everything in Common"—Com-
    munism—to suffer a significant setback.

From the Slavish people [Russia] will come
    songs, slogans and threats
But then their Leaders and Statesmen placed
    in prisons,
The pronouncement of these headless idiots
Will be received as divine utterances.

A major point made here by Nostradamus is that
at sometime during an Easter season, there will be
a major upheaval in the government of the Soviet
Union. Rising demands for consumer goods as
produced in the capitalist nations, combined with
a resurgence of old-fashioned nationalism among
the minorities of the country, will force the old
Stalinist dictators from the Kremlin. It will result
in the establishment of a new form of government
which will be Communist in name only.

In the first quatrain of this section, a more
accurate translation of the first line would be,
"The Law of More will be seen to decline," refer-
ring to the philosophy of Sir Thomas More, as
found in his book *Utopia*, published in Latin in
1516 and undoubtedly read by Nostradamus while
he was still a schoolboy. Any of the psychic's
contemporaries would undoubtedly connect the
"Law of More" with Communism. Many prominent literary sources class More's *Utopia* along with
Plato's *Republic* and the writings of Bacon as the
ancestor of the modern ideology of Communism.

NOSTRADAMUS PREDICTS

Comments Edgar Leoni as quoted in Stewart Robb's *Strange Prophecies that Came True*, p. 146,

For the reader in the second half of the 20th century, this is one of the most interesting of all the prophecies of Nostradamus—one full of potent meaning for this era, after having had none from the 16th to the 20th centuries. We now have the generic name, "Communism" to apply to the Utopian ideologies of which Sir Thomas More's *Utopia* is the common ancestor . . . The prophecy implies a widespread success of this ideology prior to its decline, and mentions that the decline will start where the Dnieper is located. This is the principal river of the Ukraine. In Nostradamus's day it was one of the most backward parts of Europe, part of the Polish-Lithuanian state for three hundred years, and hardly an area Nostradamus would choose for the locale involving any contemporary movement of this nature, such as the Anabaptists. Accordingly, it is not unreasonable to speculate on a possible twentieth-century fulfillment of this prophecy, involving the Soviet Ukraine and perhaps its chief city (which is on the Dnieper), Kiev. The nature of the more seductive and the more attractive tongue are subjects for further speculation.

From the context of the verse, it is implied that this ideology would not remain in theory, but would eventually be put into practice, and have some degree of acceptance before, as the first line

16

reads, the Moricque law "will be seen to decline." The twentieth-century fulfillment of the first part of this prediction—with a full one-third of the world today living under some form of Communism—needs no elaboration.

A surprising element in this prognostication of Nostradamus is his designation of the place where the future decline of Communism is to take place. "The Boristhenes first will come to give way," he proclaimed unhesitantly. The river that used to be known as Boristhenes is the modern Dnieper, one of the three prominent rivers of the Russian heartland, the Ukraine. Not even in his wildest dreams did Karl Marx imagine that this backward area of the country would be the first to experiment with proletariat dictatorship. Yet this is exactly what eventually happened.

Nostradamus's use of the Dnieper may have meant several things. Today, the Ukraine is one of Russia's trouble spots of nationalism and unrest, and perhaps it will be among the Ukrainians that a second Russian revolution will begin. It is more likely however, that the psychic used the Dnieper as a synecdoche to represent Russia as a whole. Kiev, once the capital of Russia, is situated on the banks of the Dnieper, and perhaps equally as important is the fact that the headwaters of the river have their source at the foot of the Valdai Hills in the Smolensk region, not all that far from present-day Moscow. Consequently, whether we want to use sixteenth-century terminology or prefer to put it in twentieth-century words, the seer's use of Boristhenes has all the appearance of symbolizing the government of Russia.

Q5. Friendship Between the United States and Russia

Un jour seront d'amis les deux grand maîtres
Leur grand pouvoir se verra augmenté:
La terre neuve sera en ses hauts êtres,
Au sanguinaire le nombre raconté. (II,89)

One day two great masters will be friends,
Their great power will be increased,
The New World will then be at its high peak,
To the bloody one will the number of dead
    be determined.

At the point in history when the United States will be the most powerful nation in the world, it will ally itself with the power of the Soviet Union. It may be the result of a realization on both sides that neither can win a war against the other, and that a form of friendship and mutual assistance may be the only way to stop the arms race. Nostradamus appears to indicate that a war could mean mutual destruction, and that because of this an alliance will be forged.

Q6. A Coming Unification in Asia

Tant attendu ne reviendra jamais,
Dedans l'Europe en Asie apparaîtra;
Un de la ligue issu du grand Hermès,
Et sur tous Rois des Orients croîtra. (X,75)

The long awaited one will never come
Into Europe; instead he will appear in Asia.

THE END OF THE WORLD

One issued from the great leagues of Hermes
[Greek god of negotiation]
He will dominate over all the Rulers of the
Orient.

The alliance between the United States and the
Soviet Union will not have any measurable result,
and the attempts to solve the differences between
the nations through international cooperation will
fail. But this will not be the case in the Far East
where a great power will succeed through negotiation and pressure to unify the Far Eastern nations
under its leadership.

Q7. Divisions Among the Races

Un peu de temps les temples des couleurs
De blanc et noir des deux extremêlées:
Rouges et jaunes leur embleront les leurs,
Sang, terre, peste, faim, feu d'eau affolée.
  (VI,10)

In a short time the temples will be colored
In white and black, the two intermingled:
Red and yellow will make off with their
  possessions,
Blood, earth, plague, hunger, fire and mad-
  dening thirst.

The growth of the Far Eastern power will begin to
disturb the attempts at international cooperation
and friendship, for gazing into the future, Nostradamus begins to see a total breakdown in interna-

tional relations. The United Nations and similar international organizations will begin to break up and disintegrate because of racial differences and power struggles. The red and yellow races—Middle East and Far East—will walk out of the international forums, and will attempt to settle their differences by force, resulting in bloodshed, disease, famine, fires and floods; the beginning of the Holocaust.

Q8. A Meteor Strikes Earth

La grande montagne ronde de sept stades,
Après paix, guerre, faim, inondation,
Roulera loin abîmant grands contrades,
Mêmes antiques, et grande fondation. (I.69)

A great spherical mountain [a meteor] about one mile in diameter,
When peace gives way to war, famine and flooding,
Will roll end over end, then sink great nations,
Many of ancient origin; of great age.

Around the same time when peace is seriously being threatened by the developing war in the Far East, a meteor will appear and plunge into the Indian Ocean with devastating effects, creating tidal waves that will seriously affect the surrounding nations. East Africa, Australia and Southern Asia will feel the destructive power of this unearthly giant, adding to the confusion that had already been created by the cries for war.

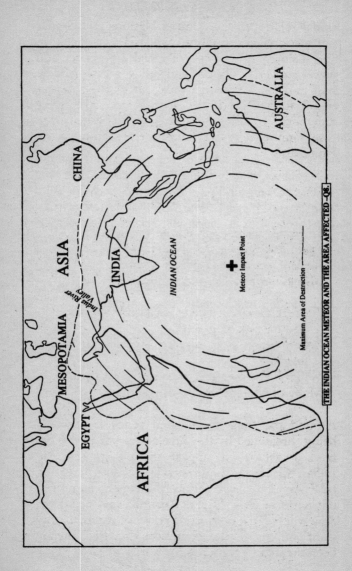

THE INDIAN OCEAN METEOR AND THE AREA AFFECTED -Q6.

In his own unexplainable way, Nostradamus describes the meteor as a "great round mountain" and furthermore gives its size as "seven stades." This description and size does not leave much to one's imagination, for the stade was the Greek foot-measure, which varied in length from time to time and place to place in the ancient world, usually measured somewhere between 607 and 738 feet. Seven stades would make the "round mountain" approximately one mile in diameter. We refer to the "mountain" as a "meteor," and the third line of the quatrain definitely points toward that conclusion, for it mentions that the "mountain" will "roll end over end," and that in its revolving motion it will "sink great countries."

The interesting fact here is that many other psychics, such as the modern-day Jeane Dixon, have made similar predictions. Says she,

I have seen a comet strike our earth around the middle of the 1980s. Earthquakes and tidal waves will befall us as the result of the tremendous impact of this heavenly body in one of our great oceans. It may well become known as one of the worst disasters of the twentieth century.

While Jeane Dixon does not name the specific nations that will be affected, Nostradamus is much more specific, and states bluntly that "many of ancient origin; of great age" will experience the wrath of the comet. History reveals that the civilizations of great age centered around the Nile in Egypt, in the Mesopotamian river valley of present-

day Iraq, and at Mohenjo-Daro on the Indus river.
A glance at a world map readily reveals that each
of these areas borders on, or is in close proximity
to, the waters of the Indian Ocean.

Suddenly the international scene changes, for
the disease, famine, fires and floods that resulted
from the emerging wars in the Far East after the
break-up of the international organizations are now
being complicated by the effects of the tidal waves.
The end-result of all this will be a weakening of
the military power of southern Asia—especially
China's adversary, India—that will open up the
way for eventual domination and consolidation
with Far Eastern expansionists.

Q9–10. A Powerful Dictator Dominates the Middle East.

Il entera vilain, mechant, infame,
Tyrannisant la Mesopotamie:
Tous amis fait d'adulterine dame,
Terre horrible noir de physionomie. (VIII,70)

Le Prince Arabe Mars, Sol, Venus, Lion,
Regne d'Église par. mer succombera:
Devers la Perse bien près d'un million,
Bisance, Egypte, ver serp invadera. (V,25)

One who is ugly, wicked and infamous will
    come to power,
And tyrannize all of Mesopotamia.
He will make friends by seducing them,

And the lands will be made horribly black by
  destruction.

The Prince of the Arabs, when Mars, the
  Sun and Venus are in Leo,
Will make the rule of the Church suffer at
  sea.
Towards Iran nearly a million men will
  march,
The true serpent will also invade Turkey and
  Egypt.

While the Far East is still in the throes of the
after-effects of the destruction wrought by the mete-
orite and the social and economic uncertainty that
resulted from the actions of the Far Eastern expansionists, another move of great significance is taking place in the Middle East. Nostradamus "sees"
an Arab leader of questionable reputation come to
power and strengthen his political power with military force. This man, whose power will initially
only be felt with a tyrannizing brutality in the
countries of Syria, Iraq and Jordan (the area of
old Mesopotamia), will mount an army of close
to a million men and march into Iran, Turkey
and Egypt, while he will simultaneously strike
a blow against the Roman Catholic Church
through an "act at sea." Nostradamus does not
leave any doubt about the timing of this daring
act. The astrological configuration as given by
him points to 2 August 1987. At this point,
however, he does not elaborate on the nature of
the attack.

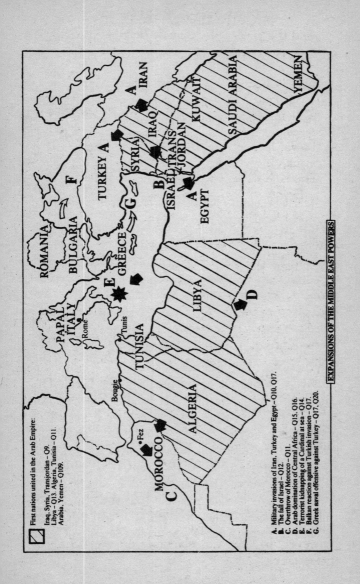

First nations united in the Arab Empire:
Iraq, Syria, Transjordan – Q9.
Libya – Q13. Algeria, Tunisia – Q11.
Arabia, Yemen - Q109.

A. Military invasions of Iran, Turkey and Egypt – Q10. Q17.
B. The fall of Israel – Q12.
C. Overthrow of Morocco – Q11.
D. Arab domination of Central Africa – Q15. Q16.
E. Terrorist kidnapping of a Cardinal at sea – Q14.
F. Balkan reaction against Turkish invasion – Q17.
G. Greek naval offensive against Turkey – Q17. Q20.

EXPANSIONS OF THE MIDDLE EAST POWERS

Q11. Muslim Unification in North Africa

Au point du jour au second chant du coq,
Ceux de Tunes, de Fez, et de Bugie,
Par les Arabes captif le Roi Maroq,
L'an mil six cent et sept, de Liturgie. (VI,54)

At daybreak, at the second crowing of the cock,
Those of Tunis [Tunisia], of Fez, [north Morocco], and Bougie [Algeria]
By these Arabs, the King of Morocco will be captured
Sixteen hundred and seven years after the development of the Liturgie. (AD35–375)

By now the entire area of the Middle East and North Africa stands ablaze, for Arab forces based in Tunisia and Algeria and guerilla forces from northern Morocco will invade the pro-Western monarchy of Morocco and overthrow its king. The development of the Liturgie, used as the basis for his time reckoning, took place over a period of nineteen years, beginning in AD 355, and Nostradamus therefore predicts the invasion to take place sometime between 1962 and 1981, although the *refinement* of the Liturgie took several more years, making it very possible that the attack will take place some time after 1981. It will however, according to his forecast, occur in the second hour after the break of dawn; i.e. an early morning surprise attack.

Q12. The Fall of Israel to the Arabs

La synagogue stérile sans nul fruit
Sera reçue entre les infidèles:
De Babylon la fille du poursuit,
Misère et triste lui tranchera les ailes. (VIII,96)

The Synagogue [the Jerusalem "temple"] ster-
   ile, and without bearing fruit,
Will be received into the hands of the infidels
   [Muslims].
The daughter of the persecuted exiles of Bab-
   ylon [Israel]
Will be miserable and sad because her wings
   of flight shall be clipped.

The Arab attacks on their neighbors will also be
directed against the State of Israel, which will end
up being defeated by the Arab armies, since it
never possessed the spirituality of Israel of old.
The final blow to the State of Israel will come
when she finds her airforce defeated, leaving her
totally at the mercy of the Arab conquerors.

Q13. A Libyan Leader Will Cause Confusion

Prince Libyque puissant en Occident
Français d'Arabe viendra tant enflammer.
Savant aux lettres sera condescendant
La langue Arabe en Français translater. (III,27)

A Libyan Prince [ruler] will become influen-
   tial in the West [Europe]

27

And will create much tension between the
French and the Arabs.
Well versed, he will cause trouble
By his interpretation of Arabian into French.

Whether it will be done on purpose or not, Nostradamus predicts that a Libyan leader will inflame the already tense situation even more by mistranslating important messages between the Arabs and the Europeans, infuriating both the Arabs and the French.

Q14. Kidnapping by Arab Terrorists

Par mer le rouge sera pris de pirates,
La paix sera par son moyen troublée:
L'ire et l'avare commettra par feint acte,
Au grand Pontife sera l'armee doublée. (V,44)

On the sea, a "red one" [Cardinal] will be
taken by pirates
Because of this action peace will even be
more threatened
Through a feigned act, he will reveal his
captors' anger and greed
The great Pontiff will double his armies.

By now the series of military successes will have greatly increased the arrogance and recklessness of the Arab Powers and they will commit an act of aggression against the Roman Catholic Church, by kidnapping a Cardinal traveling by sea. He in turn will call their bluff and expose his kidnappers' temperament. Nostradamus frequently used the phrase "red ones" to denote Cardinals of the Church. By "pirates," on the other hand, the French seer meant the Muslim corsairs of North Africa who greatly hindered traffic through the Mediterranean in his time. It is obvious therefore that he means a Cardinal will be kidnapped and held at sea by Arabs. In the vernacular of the twentieth century we would identity these kidnappers as terrorists.

But how can the "great Pontiff" double his armies while in reality he has no army at all, for his Swiss guard can most certainly not be regarded as such. This reference is puzzling indeed, because although it makes sense in terms of the sixteenth century it is completely out of line in our century. In the sixteenth century the Papacy ruled over the territories of the Papal States, situated in central Italy, and had a standing army of its own. Both of these—the states *and* the army—were lost in the unification of Italy in 1870, and all that the Vatican controls right now is only the fraction of a square mile of Vatican City. However, this is not necessarily permanent. At present Italy is playing a careful balancing act between the Italian Communist Party—the largest in Western Europe—on the one hand, and the Catholic and other political parties on the other hand. If a major political breakdown in the Italian government were to occur, it is conceivable that the Church of Rome would step in believing itself forced to take over the reins of government. At least one modern "prophet," the Californian seer Criswell, has predicted that Italy will soon become a Papal State anew as the result of a new anti-Communist drive in that country. If that should happen, then the Pope will once again have a standing fighting force at his disposal. As shown in a previous Nostradamian prediction (Q10), this event will be contemporaneous with a unification of all Arab nations in the Middle East and Africa. If the Pope were indeed in control of Italy, he would certainly increase the size of the armed forces of the country against the new unified Power—especially since that Power had kidnapped an official of the Church of Rome.

Q15. Political Realignments in the East

Mer par solaires sûre ne passera,
Ceux de Venus tiendront toute l'Affrique:
Leur regne plus Saturne n'occupera,
Et changera la part Asiatique. (V,11)

Those of the Sun [the Church] will not travel
    the sea in safety,
Those of Crescent Venus [the Arab powers]
    will hold all of Africa.
Saturn [decadent forces] will no longer occupy
    their realm,
And portions of Asia will be changed the
    same way.

The increasing Arab strength and the kidnapping of a Prince of the Church will make the Church realize that the sealanes are no longer safe for their people. By now it has become extremely dangerous to travel in the Mediterranean Sea. The Arabs in the meantime are proceeding to consolidate their power throughout North Africa and even southern Africa by defeating or outsting pro-Western leaders (Q10,Q11). At the same time a similar program of "unification" will be taking place in Asia under the Oriental leader.

Q16. The Nations of Africa Align with the Middle East

Plus ne sera le grand en faux sommeil,
L'inquiétude viendra prendre repos:
Dresser phalange d'or, azur, et vermeil,
Subjuguer Afrique la ronger jusqu'os. (V,69)

No longer will the great leader be pacified,
And uneasiness will replace tranquility.
A force of gold, [yellow], azure [blue] and
    vermilion [red] will be organized,
In order to conquer Africa and exploit it to
    the fullest.

By now, the raging conquests by the Arabs are beginning to reach beyond their boundaries. Great dissatisfaction is beginning to show within the Arab leadership, and in order to satisfy their Leader's desire for power the armies now begin to threaten central and southern Africa (Q15) into alliances favorable to the Middle East.

While there are many different interpretations of the prophecies found in the biblical Book of Revelation, there are some verses in chapter 9 of this prophetic book that appear to refer to the same event, describing the same forces that will be unleashed under the biblical prophecy of the Sixth Trumpet.

And the sixth angel sounded, and I heard a voice from the four corners of the golden altar which is before God.

Saying to the sixth angel which had the trumpet, "Loose the four angels which are bound in the great Euphrates."

And the four angels were loosed, which were prepared for an hour, and a day, and a month, and a year, for to slay the third part of men.

And the army of the horsemen were two hundred thousand thousand [200-million]: and I heard the number of them.

And thus I saw the horses in vision, and them that sat on them, having breastplates of fire [red], and a jacinth [blue], and brimstone [yellow]: and the heads of the horses were as the heads of lions: and out of their mouths issued fire and smoke and brimstone.

By these three was the third part of men killed, by the fire and by the smoke and by the brimstone which issued out of their mouths.

For their power was in their mouth, and in their tails: for their tails were like unto serpents, and had heads, and with them they do hurt. (Rev. 9:13–19).

This prophecy brings out the following points:

1) The destructive forces originate from the area of the River Euphrates—the Middle East.

2) The warriors mentioned here are to be

200-million strong—a military number that has become possible only in recent times through various military alliances.

3) They are described as "horsemen" but their horses are by no means ordinary, for they have lion heads and smoking mouths. They appear to be some form of war vehicle that shoots fire and smoke—missiles perhaps.

4) Of particular interest are the dominant colors in which this destructive force is arrayed: *red, blue* and *yellow*; the same colors that appear in Nostradamian predictions.

Is it possible that these two forecasts predict the same event—a future war of unknown dimensions? In that case, how are we to regard the statement that it is "to slay the third part of men." Does this indeed indicate that the Holocaust will destroy a full one-third of all mankind; that a billion-and-a-half of this world's population will not survive?

Q17. *The Conflict Spreads into Turkey*

La grande Arabe marchera bien avant,
Trahi sera par les Bisantinois:
L'antique Rodes lui viendra au-devant,
Et plus grand mal par austre Pannonois. (V,47)

The great Arab will march on
But his ambitions will be undermined by the
    Turks.
Ancient Rhodes [the Greek navy] will move
    against him

And harm will threaten him from the Pannonians [the Balkan nations].

The Arab thrust into Turkey (Q10) will be followed by attacks by the Greek navy on their positions in order to contain their expansionist moves. The Balkan nations on the Black Sea—Romania and Bulgaria—will also threaten war when the Arabs cut off the Bosphorus Straits, interfering with commercial ships and fleet movements.

Q18–19. An Earthquake Shakes Greece and Turkey

Mars et Mercure, et l'argent joint ensemble,
Vers le midi extrème siccité:
Au fond d'Asie on dira terre tremble,
Corinthe, Ephese lors en perplexité. (III,3)

Dans plusieurs nuits la terre tremblera:
Sur le printemps deux efforts suite:
Corinthe, Ephese aux deux mers nagera:
Guerre s'émeut par deux vaillans de luite.
  (II,52)

Mars, Mercury and the moon joined together,
In southern lands [Africa and south Asia] there
  will be extreme drought.
Beneath Asia the earth will tremble,
Affecting Corinth [Greece] and Ephesus
  [Turkey].

For several nights the earth will continue to
  shake,

And in the spring there will be two shocks in
   succession.
When Corinth and Ephesus will meet on the
   seas,
War will erupt between these two valiant warring nations.

At that moment, while the area erupts into open
hostility and Greece and Turkey exacerbate their
differences by attempting to fight in a major sea
battle, a series of tremendous earthquakes and
aftershocks originating in Central Asia will cause
destruction throughout the two warring nations.
In this prediction Nostradamus is joined by Jeane
Dixon who says that: "Sometime around the middle of the 1980s—in fact, I feel that it will be in
the year 1985," she says, "nature will interfere
with the Soviet plan for world conquest. In that
year there will be a natural phenomenon which
will cause profound changes in the events shaping
the course of humanity—a natural phenomenon of
the first order."

*Q20–Q21. The Defeat of the Greeks and the Fall of
Cyprus*

Les Rhodiens demanderont secours,
Par le neglect de ses hoirs delaissée.
L'empire Arabe révélera son cours,
Par Hesperies la cause redressée (IV, 39)

En ce temps là sera frustrée Cypres,
De son secours de ceux de mer Egee:

NOSTRADAMUS PREDICTS

Vieux trucides: mais par mesles et lyphres
Séduit leur Roi, Reine plus outragée. (III,89)

The Rhodians [the Greek navy] will call for
  assistance,
But they will be abandoned by their leaders.
The Arab empire will now reveal its intentions,
And Hesperia [Land to the far west—America?]
will compensate for the losses.

At that time Cyprus will be frustrated
For not receiving relief from those of the
  Aegean Sea [the Greeks]
The Old Ones will be slaughtered [defeated]
  by cannon balls and demands,
And the Ruler capitulates and his wife is
  outraged.

It appears that the Greek navy will suffer great
losses, not only against the Turks but against the
Arabs as well, for they are now showing their true
intentions. Their urgent plea for reinforcement falls
on deaf ears, for the nation simply has no rein-
forcements to commit to the battle. Realizing
this, the Arabs openly announce their continued
aggression while the United States resupplies
the Greek navy. It will not, however, stem the
tide, and after the Greek positions on the island
of Cyprus have been overrun, the Cypriots surrender—much to the indignation of the Cypriot
leader's wife.

Q22. A Military Alliance Between the United States and Russia

Quand ceux du pôle arctique unis ensemble,
En Orient grand effrayeur et crainte:
Élu nouveau, soutenu le grand tremble,
Rhodes, Bisance de sang Barbare teinté. (VI,21)

When those of the Arctic Pole are united together
There will be great terror and fear in the Orient.
The newly elected leader, though strongly supported, will tremble
While at the same time Rhodes [Greece] and Turkey will be stained with Arab blood.

At approximately the same time as the war between Greece and Turkey is being fought and the Arab forces invade Turkey, (Q10,Q20), the two nations who share communication across the Arctic Ocean—the United States and the Soviet Union—will announce or conclude a military alliance against the Far Eastern power and the consolidated Arab forces. This will cause grave concern in the Far East, and the newsly elected leader of the Far Eastern alliance will have much to fear.

Q23. The United States Threatens the East with War

De l'aquatique triplicité naîtra
D'un qui fera le jeudi pour sa fête:
Son bruit, los, regne, sa puissance croîtra,
Par terre et mer aux Orients tempête. (I,50)

Of the three waters there will be born
One that will make Thursday its holiday.
Its fame, praise, rule and power will grow,
By land and sea. It will appear as a tempest to
    the Orient.

This quatrain is one of the most interesting—
especially for the United States, for here we have
a cryptic description of a nation which, according
to the last line, will someday become a "tempest
to the Orient." The first specific point as to its
identity is that it will arise out of "three waters";
that is, it will be a nation surrounded on three
sides by water. This could be an allusion to any
number of nations.

The second characteristic, however, reduces the
possibilities to only one: Thursday, according to
Nostradamus, would be the day of celebration
unique to this enigmatic nation. Of all nations in
existence today, only the United States has a
national Thursday holiday—Thanksgiving Day—
which by a decree of a joint resolution of the
United States Congress in 1941 was specified to
be celebrated on the fourth Thursday of every
November. Later, Canada also instituted a Thanksgiving Day, but their holiday falls on a Monday.
The United States is unique in respect of its Thursday holiday.

But there is more.

The United States also fits the first characteristic, for it is surrounded by three bodies of water—
the Atlantic, the Pacific and the Gulf of Mexico.
Nostradamus also depicted the Thursday-keeping
nation to grow in "fame, praise, rule and power."

The phenomenal rise of the United States to be a first-rate power in its two hundred years of development needs no special elaboration. As to the last characteristic which holds that the nation described would be a tempest by land and sea against the Orient, it would appear at first glance that the United States fulfilled this point during World War II. In fact, Nostradamus hit on the exact time period, for the Congressional resolution instituting Thanksgiving was made in 1941— the same year as the attack on Pearl Harbor by the Japanese fleet, and the beginning of the US war in the Pacific.

But the prophet's use of the word "Orient" usually meant an area much larger than just the Far East. The way he used it took in all the East, including the Middle East. If this is what he really had in mind, then the last line has yet to be more completely fulfilled, suggesting that America will still become involved in a coming conflict that will involve almost all of Asia.

Q24. The Breakdown of Peace Negotiations at Geneva

Du lac Leman les sermons fâcheront,
Des jours seront réduits par des semaines,
Puis mois, puis ans, puis tous défailliront,
Les Magistrats damneront leur lois vaines. (I,47)

The deliberations from the Lake of Geneva
   will be annoying.
They will stretch over days, weeks,

Months and even years, and in the end they
    will fail,
The world leaders will damn their useless
    decisions.

Although the Arab powers and the Far Eastern
expansionists keep their areas in a constant state
of agitation, attempts at finding a peaceful solution have been conducted unceasingly, but to no
avail. The Geneva talks will finally come to an
end; not with peace as the ultimate result, but
with the conviction that peace is totally unat-
tainable.

War—global war—seems to be unavoidable.

The stage has been set for an all-destroying
Holocaust.

Chapter 2

NUCLEAR WAR—AND THE FAR EASTERN ADVANCE

Q25. *China Launches a Surprise Nuclear Attack*

Soleil levant un grand feu l'on verra,
Bruit et clarté vers Aquilon tendants:
Dedans le rond mort et cris l'on ouira,
Par glaive, feu, faim, mort les attendants. (II,91)

At sunrise one will see a great fire,
The noise and light will be aimed toward
   Aquilon [nations of the far north]
Within the lands of the Arctic Circle one will
   hear cries of death
Through instruments of steel, death will come
   through fire and famine.

While no one knows how a future war will really develop and what the moves will be that will introduce or necessitate the use of nuclear weapons, Nostradamus's predictions are loaded with ominous words and phrases that appear to warn of nuclear destruction.

What he predicted for Aquilon in this quatrain is very ominous indeed. The key to this quatrain is the decipherment of the proper name Aquilon in the second line. Aquilon is derived from the Latin *aquilo*, or north. In his "Epistle to Henri II," in which the seer summarized some of his predictions of the future, Nostradamus described what he called the "lords of Aquilon, two in number" who shall become "brothers" and as a result of their combined force, "all the Orient shall tremble." Those two lords/brothers of Aquilon are identical in description to the "two great masters" of Q5, and to "those of the Arctic Pole [North] united together" who will cause "great terror and fear in the Orient" of Q22. These were identified as the future Russian-American alliance. Aquilon symbolizes the same.

The nuclear attack will come suddenly and take the lords of Aquilon by surprise.

While the nations are still asleep, during the early morning hours, "one will see a great fire" emerge out of nowhere. Inasmuch as the seer indicates that the "noise and light" will be aimed toward Aquilon, we may assume that it does not originate in either of the Aquilon powers but will be aimed at them from somewhere else. The effects of this strange and unexpected attack will be devastating. The third line of the quatrain specifies that "Within the circle one will hear cries of death": "Within the circle" can only refer to "those of the Arctic Pole" of Q22; the circle being the Arctic Circle. In the area enclosed with this geographic

THE CHINESE GERM ATTACK AGAINST THE ARCTIC AND ITS EXTENT

circle "one will hear cries of death," caused by the "steel instruments" that will cause "fire" [immediate effects] and "famine" [long-range effects].

What Nostradamus might have been hinting at is nothing less than a nuclear attack on the United States and Russia, and its terrible results. Yet the attack will not be the result of a clash between these two powers, but will be launched by a third unidentified party that hurls "steel instruments" of "noise and lighting" [ICBMs?] toward Russia and the United States. In reference to Nostradamus's developing scenario of a war between East and West, the only nation that has full nuclear capability beside the USA and Russia and is able to wage a nuclear war is Red China, the Giant of the East.

Q26–Q28. The Atomic Destruction

Sera laissé feu vif, mort caché,
Dedans les globes horrible epouvantable,
De nuit à classe cité en poudre lâché,
La cité à feu, l'ennemi favourable. (V,8)

L'an que Saturne et Mars égaux combust,
L'air fort séché longue trajection:
Par feux secrets d'ardeur grand lieu adust,
Peu pluie, vent chaud, guerres, incursions.
(IV,67)

De nuit Soleil penseront avoir vu
Quand le pourceau demi-homme on verra:
Bruit, chant, bataille, au ciel battre aperçu,
Et bêtes brutes à parler l'on orra. (I,64)

THE END OF THE WORLD

There will be unleashed a live force, a secret
    form of death,
Horrible and frightful. It will be contained in
    globes.
Launched from a fleet of ships, it will reduce
    a city to dust in a single night.
The city ignites; the enemy offers peace.

When Saturn and Mars [evil and war] are
    equally powerful,
The air will be made very dry because of an
    elongated shooting-star.
Through secret fires it will cause a great place
    to blaze with scorching heat,
There will be little rain [but] a hot wind
    during war and invasions.

Many will think they see the sun at night,
They shall also see deformed men, half-animal,
    and half-human.
Noise, sounds, battles, and fighting in the
    sky will be seen,
And one will hear strange beasts talking
    [radio?].

Does this *really* need an explanation or an "interpretation?" It is uncanny how this ancient seer
could give such an accurate description of a modern nuclear attack without having read about the
destruction of Hiroshima and Nagasaki. But the
ferocious attack of the East against the nations of
Aquila will not be limited to nuclear warfare alone.
It has other, even more frightening, dimensions.

Q29. *Germ Warfare Launched Against the Arctic*

Si grande famine par onde pestifère,
Par pluie longue le long du pôle arctique:
Samarobryn cent lieues de l'hémisphere,
Vivront sans loi exempt de politique (VI,5)

A great famine will be caused by a disease-
producing wave
It will be carried by a lengthy rain, coming
from the Arctic Pole.
At the same time, a winged satellite will
orbit 270 miles above the earth,
When there will be no politics or existing
under the laws of others.

The Easterners, not satisfied with the wholesale
slaughter caused by their nuclear attack, will seed
the Arctic skies with deadly bacteria. Carried by
the wind and rain the disease will spread southward across Canada, the United States, Russia
and northern Europe. Information contained in
the quatrain suggests that the attack will originate
from a space platform orbiting 270 miles above
Earth. The rules of the Geneva Convention will
be completely ignored, with citizens as well as the
military suffering from the effects.

The first two lines of this verse seem to be a
repeat of the picture given in Q25. Again, a
famine is mentioned, and it is associated with the
Arctic Pole. However it is described as a "very
great famine" and it comes as the result of a
"pestiferous" or "disease-producing wave," descend-
ing to earth through a "lengthy rain."

THE END OF THE WORLD

What is portrayed here could at first glance appear to be the long-range effects of radiation from the nuclear attack described in Q25. But it could also be a prediction of the use of another, more diabolical weapon. Washington seeress Jeane Dixon has predicted that the Chinese will indeed make use of germ warfare during the next major war. If this is what Nostradamus was hinting at in this quatrain, it means that the Chinese will specifically use bacteriological weapons in the Arctic. In this way the Chinese would be able to cripple the Western Allies severely in one effective blow, for the Arctic is a barometric high-pressure region where storms originate and move southward throughout the entire northern hemisphere. A heavy seeding of the polar atmosphere with a type of bacteria that uses moisture as a carrier, would result in a spreading of the disease by storm clouds, dispersing them "through a lengthy rain" throughout the United States, Russia, England, Europe—China's major adversaries. *China, on the other hand, would not be affected because its weather originates with the monsoons coming from the south.*

It is interesting to note that two modern-day psychic seers, Jeane Dixon and Edgar Cayce, have emphasized that the Davis Strait, located between Baffin Island and Greenland, is to become what they call a life-line between two nations. The only way the Davis Strait could gain such a strategic importance would be through the arising of an urgent need for a direct route of travel between the United States and Canada and Russia across the Arctic. Can it be that the Chinese germ attack will be part of a tactic to cut this communications route?

The quatrains of Nostradamus dealing with this attack reveal much more than the obvious wording. The third line of the verse alludes to the spot from where the bacteriological warfare attack will originate. A strict translation of the original French reads: "Samarobryn one hundred leagues from the hemisphere" and these words contain some of the most informative information of the quatrain.

1) "Samarobryn *one hundred leagues* from the hemisphere."

How much or rather how *far* is "one hundred leagues?" In sixteenth-century Europe, the measure of a league varied considerably, from 2.5 miles to as much as 4.5 miles. In another of his prophecies, however, Nostradamus makes mention of a convent named Saint-Paul-de Mausole, situated just outside the seer's birthplace at St. Rémy in southern France, and described it as being "three leagues from the Rhône." By modern measurement, the convent is a fraction over eight miles from the banks of the Rhône, making Nostradamus's three leagues close to 2.7 miles each. *Based on this, "one hundred leagues" would be equivalent to 270 miles.*

2) "Samarobryn one hundred leagues *from the hemisphere.*"

This is a most interesting and accurate phrase, because in order to be 270 miles from all points of the "hemisphere" of Earth, one would have to be orbiting at that distance out in space. In modern astronautical terms, in fact, Nostradamus's use of the word hemisphere is correct, since someone or something a certain distance away from Earth on one side would be that much further away from the other side of the globe at any given moment.

3) "*Samorobryn* one hundred leagues from the hemisphere."

The word samarobryn is composed of two parts: a) *samara,* or seed-pod, and b) a form of the Latin verb *obire.* The latter of these means to wander, to travel, also to *encircle;* and as an intransitive verb it is used specifically to describe a celestial object, *something which has the appearance of a heavenly body setting in the sky.* As to the description of the object itself, *samara* may be a clue. For Samara is a seed from an ash, elm or maple tree and is composed of a central pod with either one or two projecting wings.

Putting these various elements together, we get the distinct impression that Nostradamus was attempting to picture an object spherical in shape with an outer shell, having wing projections, and circling Earth at an altitude of 270 miles. In modern terms, this is very probably a satellite or space platform with one or two solar panels.

It is perhaps significant that China has not yet agreed to the banning of offensive weapons from space. There is no doubt that sometime during the 1980s, China will attain the capability of launching sophisticated orbiting platforms and stations. We must also realize that although our technology enables us to know whether a satellite is armed with nuclear weapons this capability does not exist when it comes to ascertaining whether or not an orbiting platform carries bacteriological weapons. The Chinese may well take advantage of this.

Q30. The Chinese Invasion of Southern France

Du pont Euxine, et la grand Tartarie,
Un roi sera qui viendra voir la Gaule,
Transpercera Alane et l'Armenie,
Et dedans Bisance lairra sanglante Gaule. (V,54)

From beyond the Black Sea and Mongolia
  [China]
There will be a King who will travel in the
  direction of France,
He will pierce through Alania and Armenia
  [southern Russia]
And in Turkey he will leave the mark of his
  bloody rod.

During the devastation wrought by their atomic
attack on the polar region or shortly thereafter,
the Eastern forces will launch an attack in the
direction of Europe—in the direction of France.
The Eastern commander will wipe away all resistance during his conquering sweep across southern
Russia on the way to Turkey in an endeavor to
link up with the Arabs, for a combined attack on
the Allied positions. Nostradamus advises us that
he, the commander, will be armed with a rod-
shaped weapon that will cause tremendous destruction.

Q31. Arab and Chinese Assault on Turkey

Au calmé Duc en arrachant l'esponce
Voile Arabesque voir, subit découverte:

Tripolis, Chio, et ceux de Trapesconce,
Duc pris, Marnegro et la cite déserte. (VI,55)

The duke will be appeased, and a contract of
    peace will be drawn up,
But suddenly Arab naval forces will be seen
    and discovered.
From Tripoli [Libya] they will come to Chios
    [in the Aegean], while other forces will
    appear at Trabzon [north-east Turkey]
The duke will be captured, and the Black Sea
    and the city turned into desert.

Under the threat of an all-out attack, the Turks
will sign a peace treaty with the attackers, but the
peace will be broken when from Tripoli the Arab
naval forces strike against the west coast of Turkey. Coordinated with this Arab move the Chinese army will devastate the north-east area of
Turkey by annihilating the Turkish naval forces
on the Black Sea and the coastal city of Trabzon
with the aid of nuclear weapons.

Q32–Q33. Greece Devastated by Germ Warfare

Dans les cyclades, en perinthe et larisse,
Dedans Sparte tout le Peloponnesse:
Se grande famine, peste par faux connisse,
Neuf mois tiendra et tout le chevronèse. (V,90)

L'horrible peste Perynte et Nicopolle,
Le Chersonese tiendra et Marceloyne:
La Thessalie vastera l' Amphipolle,
Mal inconnu, et le refus d' Anthoine. (IX,91)

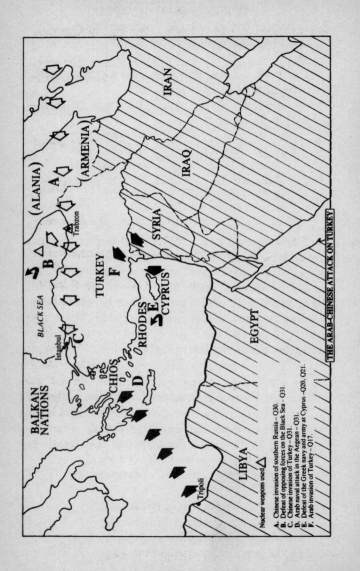

THE ARAB-CHINESE ATTACK ON TURKEY

A. Chinese invasion of southern Russia – Q30.
B. Defeat of opposing forces on the Black Sea – Q31.
C. Chinese invasion of Turkey – Q31.
D. Arab naval attack in the Aegean – Q31.
E. Defeat of the Greek navy and army at Cyprus – Q20, Q21.
F. Arab invasion of Turkey – Q17.

△ Nuclear weapons used

In the Cyclades [islands south-east of Greece],
   in Perinthus
[east Thrace], and in Larissa [north Greece],
   in Sparta and the entire Peloponnesus
   [south Greece],
Will be a year of great famine; from disease
   caused by artificial dust.
And it will last for nine months throughout
   the Grecian peninsula.

The horrible plague on Perinthus, and Nicopolis [west Greece]
In the [Peloponnesus] Peninsula and Macedonia [north-west Greece] will it fall.
It will also devastate Thessaly and Amphipolos
   [in Macedonia]
It will be an unknown evil, and from a leader
   named Anthony will come a refusal to
   help.

Having conquered Turkey, the Chinese/Arab attention is now focused on Greece and, while undoubtedly regrouping after their bloody battle for Turkey, the Eastern forces commence to unleash a
deadly attack of germ warfare against the Greeks;
the effects of which will last for at least nine
months, destroying not only the population but
the vegetation as well.

Q34. Athens Attacked from Albania

Au grand marché qu'on dit des mensongers,
Du tout Torrent et champ Athenien:

Seront surpris par les chevaux légers,
Par Albanois Mars, Leo, Sat. un versien. (V,91)

They will meet at the market place of liars,
Then through the passage to the field of
  Athens.
They will be surprised by the light vehicles
Of the Albanians, with Mars in Leo and
  Saturn in Aquarius.

After an attempt to pressure the Greeks into surrender at the negotiation table, forces from the
Chinese satellite nation of Albania will invade
Greece in a surprise attack using light-armored
vehicles.

Q35. Yugoslavia Threatened

Conflit Barbare en la cornette noire,
Sang épandu trembler la Dalmatie:
Grand Ismaël mettra son promontoire,
Ranes trembler secours Lusitanie. (IX,60)

The warring Arab will wear a black helmet,
Blood will be shed, Dalmatia [the Yugoslavian coast] will tremble.
Great Ishmael [the Arab commander?] will
  set up his observation post,
The Amphibians will tremble because of the
  aid of Portugal.

From Albania and conquered Greece, the eastern
conquerors will threaten Yugoslavia with an amphib-

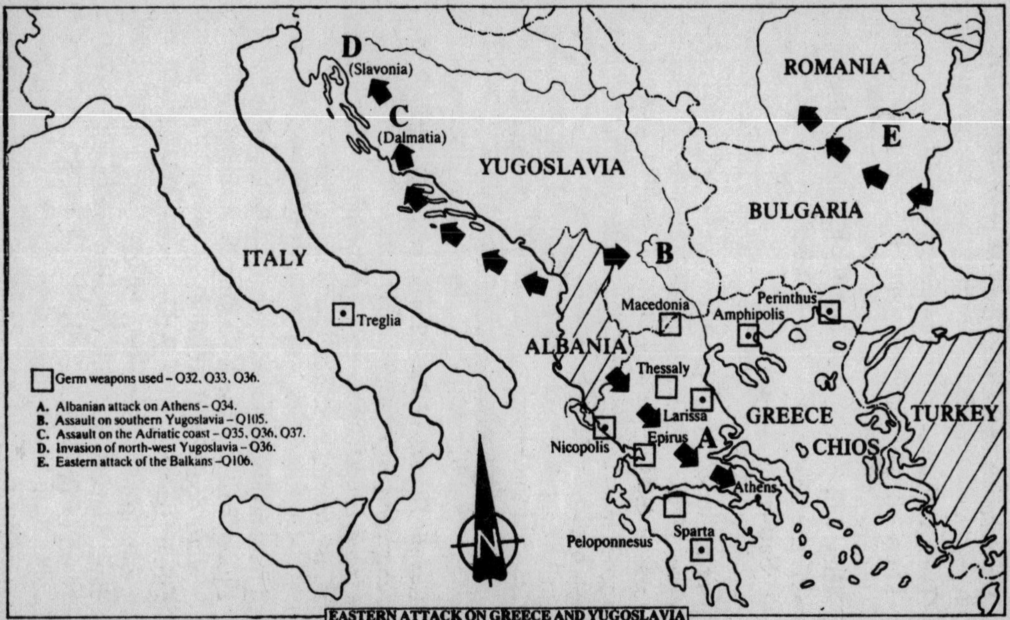
ROMANIA
YUGOSLAVIA
BULGARIA
ITALY
ALBANIA
GREECE
CHIOS
TURKEY
D
(Slavonia)
C
(Dalmatia)
B
A
E
Treglia
Macedonia
Perinthus
Amphipolis
Thessaly
Larissa
Epirus
Nicopolis
Athens
Sparta
Peloponnesus
N
Germ weapons used – Q32, Q33, Q36.
A. Albanian attack on Athens – Q34.
B. Assault on southern Yugoslavia – Q105.
C. Assault on the Adriatic coast – Q35, Q36, Q37.
D. Invasion of north-west Yugoslavia – Q36.
E. Eastern attack of the Balkans –Q106.

EASTERN ATTACK ON GREECE AND YUGOSLAVIA

ious assault, but the Eastern commander decides to delay the attack because of a Western coordinated counter-offensive that has been launched from Portugal.

Q36. Invasion of Yugoslavia; Italy Suffers Germ Warfare

Lait, sang grenouilles escoudre en Dalmatie.
Conflit donné, peste près de Balenne:
Cri sera grand par toute Esclavonia,
Lors naître monstre près et dedans Ravenne.
(II,32)

The spilling of Amphibian blood will be planned to take place in Dalmatia [Yugoslavian coast]

But conflict will be ordered, and disease will [break out] near Treglia [central south-west Italy]

A great cry will sound through all Slavonia [north Yugoslavia]

Then a monster will be seen near and within Ravenna.

The Western allies will plan a counter-attack against the Eastern invasion of the Yugoslavian coast, but the Easterners will strike before they are prepared. With relentless force the Easterners will advance into Yugoslavia and hinder Western efforts by unleashing bacteriological weapons in central Italy. A military build-up on the Italian coast in and around Ravenna will also be destroyed.

Q37. Greece and Italy Attacked at the Same Time

La gent étrange divisera butins,
Saturne et Mars son regard furieux:
Horrible estrange aux Toscans et Latins,
Grecs, qui seront à frapper curieux! (I,83)

The foreign nation will divide the spoils,
Saturn and Mars [evil and war], their aspects
    bellicose.
Horrible slaughter of the Tuscans and Latins
    [Italians]
And Greeks, whom they will strike against.

After the invasion of Greece by the Eastern forces,
they will turn their attack to Italy while at the
same time mopping up the remainder of the Greek
resistance.

Q38. Eastern Forces Prepare to Invade Italy

Entre Campaignie, Sienne, Flora, Tuscie,
Six mois neuf jours ne pleuvra une goutte:
L'étrange lange en terre Dalmatie
Courira sus, vastant la terre toute. (II,84)

Between Campania, Siena, Florence and
    Tuscany [central, south and west Italy]
Not a drop of rain will fall for six months and
    nine days
When a foreign language will be spoken in
    Dalmatia [Yugoslavia]
Soon it will overrun them; and devastate the
    entire country.

At the time when foreigners overrun Yugoslavia, a devastating drought will hit Italy and the food-producing regions will be destroyed. The numerous references to severe weather changes—lengthy rains or droughts or floods—may be indications that the Easterners will have ways of controlling the weather and use it as part of their overall strategy; as an additional weapon against their enemies.

Q39–Q40. Civil War in Italy

Crier victoire du grand Selin croissant:
Par les Romains sera l'Aigle clamé,
Ticcin, Milan et Gennes n'y consent,
Puis par eux-memes Basil grand réclamé. (VI,78)

Du haut du mont Aventin voix ouie,
Videz, videz de tous les deux côtes:
Du sang des rouges sera l'ire assomie,
D'Arimin Prato, Columna debotez. (IX,2)

In order to achieve victory over the greatly expanding Crescent [the Muslims]
The government of Rome will call for aid from the Eagle [United States].
Pavia, Milan and Genoa [north Italy] will not agree with this
They will break away, and choose their own leader.

A voice will be heard from the top of Aventine Hill [Rome]
"Be gone Be gone! All of you on both sides."

But their anger will be appeased only by the blood
of the Church leaders,
And from Rimini and Prato [north Italy], the
representatives of the Church will be expelled.

Uncertain about their fate and fearful of the attacking armies of the East, Italy will dissolve into
dissenting fractions with everyone claiming to have
another—a *better*—solution for the political problems facing the country. Rome—and we may have
to keep in mind that by this time the Catholic
Church will be in control of the country—will
demand military assistance from the United States,
but the political leaders in northern Italy will
strongly disagree. They will break away in protest
against the policies of the Church and end up
selecting their own government. The leaders in
Rome will plead with them to agree to a negotiated settlement, but the rebelling Italians in the
north will settle for nothing short of the death of
those Church leaders who control the Italian government and, to show their determination to run
their own part of Italy, they expel all priests and
Catholic officials from their region.

Q41. Subversion in the Italian Government

Lorsque soldats fureur séditieuse,
Contre leur chef feront de nuit fer luire:
Ennemi d'Albe soit par main furieuse,
Lors vexer Rome et principaux séduire (VI,68)

When rebel soldiers in a fury,

Will fight with flashing steel weapons against
  their chief
The Albanian enemy will also be working
  furiously,
And they will vex Rome by bribing the principal ones.

It now appears that the Italian civil war is secretly
backed by the Albanians and Eastern subversives
from Albania, and they will succeed in penetrating the Italian government in Rome by paying off
corrupt government officials.

Q42–Q46. The Destruction of Rome

Les Albanois passeront dedans Rome,
Moyennant Langres demipler affublés,
Marquis et Duc ne pardonnent à l'homme,
Fue, sang, morbiles point d'eau faillir les blés.
(IV,98)

Que peste et glaive n'a su definer,
Mort dans le puys sommet du ciel frappé:
L'abbé mourra quand verra ruiner,
Ceux du naufrage l'écueil voulant grapper. (II,56)

O vaste Rome ta ruines s'approche,
Non de tes murs, de ton sang et substance:
L'âpre par lettres fera si horrible coche,
Fer pointu mis à tous jusqu'au manche. (X,65)

Bien près du Tymbre presse la Libytine:
Un peu devant grande inondation:

THE END OF THE WORLD

Le chef du nef pris, mis à la sentine:
Château, palais en conflagration. (II,93)

Par gent étrange, et de Romains lointaine
Leur grande cité après eau fort troublee:
Fille sans main, trop different domaine,
Pris chef, serrure, n'avoir été riblée. (II,54)

The Albanians will come to Rome,
But the multitude will hide themselves because
  of the locusts in the sky.
The leaders will not give relief to anyone
And there will be fire, blood and disease, and
  without the rain, the crops will fail.

But neither disease nor steel weapons will
  destroy it completely.
Death will come to the top of the hills when
  they will be hit from the sky.
A Church leader will die when he realizes
  that everything has been ruined.
And those who are left attempt to find security.

O vast Rome, your ruin will approach you.
Not just your walls, but your blood and your
  substance as well.
A leader ordering the harshest commands will
  leave his horrible mark on you.
And you will receive the full measure of destruction.

Very near the Tiber [Rome] will threaten the
  Libyans
Shortly before there will be a great flood.

61

The Chief-of-State will be captured and
    imprisoned,
The Castle [San Angelo] and the Palace [the
    Vatican] will be in flames.

Because of a people who are foreigners, and
    distant to the Romans [Easterners]
Their great city will be much troubled from
    the sea.
Her power gone, her dominion utterly changed,
The Chief captive—with no escape.

By now the Eastern forces are sure enough of the
weakness and corruptness of the Italian government and they will attack from Albania and aim
at destroying the city of Rome. Aerial bombard-
ments will take its toll in blood, and attacks with
germ weapons ordered by the commanding general
of the opposing forces will spread disease throughout the city. The flooding of the Tiber and the
burning and sacking of the Castle and the Vatican
will practically coincide with the imprisonment of
the Pope as the head of the government of Italy,
and indications are that he will die a prisoner.

Q47–Q49. Military Assault on Rome and Venice

Un qui les dieux d'Annibal infernaux,
Fera renaître, effrayeur des humains
Onc plus d'horreur ni plus pire journaux
Qu'avint viendra par Babel aux Romains. (II,30)

Combien de fois prise cité solaire

THE END OF THE WORLD

Seras, changeant les lois barbares et vaines:
Ton mal s'approche: Plus seras tributaire,
Le grand Hadrie recourira tes veines. (I,8)

De L'Orient viendra le coeur Punique
Fâcher Hadrie et les hoires Romulides,
Accompagné de la classe Libyque,
Trembler Melites et proches îles vides. (I,9)

The infernal gods will cause Hannibal [the North African]
To be reborn again, a terror to all men.
Only this time the destruction will be far worse,
Than in the past; he will come against the Romans by way of Babel [Middle East powers].

How many times you will be captured, solar city [Rome]
Manipulating pagan and useless laws.
Your evil comes, you will be made subservient.
From Venice other blood will come to run through your veins.

From the Orient will come the cold-hearted,
To vex Venice and the inhabitants of Rome
They will be accompanied by the Libyan [Arab] fleet,
Malta will tremble; the neighboring isles will be emptied.

While all eyes are concentrated on the capture of the Pope and the destruction of Rome, the Arabs

63

and Chinese will also push their armor toward Venice on the north-eastern Italian coast. The attack will seem so immense that evacuation plans will be enforced as far as Malta and other central Mediterranean islands.

Nostradamus exhibits a certain feeling of pathos when he laments the capture of Rome and the destruction that it will experience. In fact, some of his quatrains—even though fragmentary—are so full of melancholy and sadness that it often seems as if he was there, witnessing the death-throes of the Seat of the Roman Catholic Church.

Q50–52. The Fall of Venice

Le grand Pilote par Rois sera mandé,
Laisser la classe pour plus haut lieu atteindre:
Sept ans après sera contrebandé,
Barbare armée viendra Venise craindre. (VI,75)

Les armes battre au ciel longue saison,
L'arbre au milieu de la cité tombé:
Verbine rogne, glaive, en face tison,
Lors le monarque d'Hadrie succombé (III,11)

Cela du reste de sang non épandu:
Venise quiert secours être donné:
Après avoir bien longtemps attendu,
Cité livrée au premier cor sonné. (IV,I)

The great Admiral will be commissioned by the Commander,
To leave his naval post for a higher position.

Seven years later he will lead a rebellion against his government.
Then Venice will fear the Arab Army.

Weapons to fight in the sky a long time,
The harbor in the middle of the city will be captured.
Instruments of steel will topple the trees and burn the face,
Then Venice will fall.

In order that those who survive should not be killed,
Venice will call for aid,
But after waiting in vain for a long time,
The city will surrender at the first sound of the horn.

The Battle for Venice will come at a time of great confusion in the city, for a prominent Italian leader will rebel against the government and foment a civil war. For quite some time the Italian air force will repel the attacking armies, but eventually Eastern forces will be able to penetrate to within the center of the city and destroy it with a blast that will burn the trees and damage the face of the city. The Venetians wait in vain for the expected aid but when all their pleas go unheeded, the city will be surrendered to the enemy.

Q53–Q54. France Enters the War

Si France passe outre mer lygustique,

A. Attack on Rome and Venice – Q42-Q52.
B. French fleets defeated in the Adriatic and Mediterranean – Q53, Q54, Q69.
C. Penetration up the River Po – Q58.
D. French army defeats near Rome, Ancona and Ravenna-Modena – Q60, Q61, Q70.
E. Sea attacks against the Italian west coast and Sicily – Q67-Q70, Q230.
F. Attack on Sardinia and Corsica – Q69, Q71.
G. French defeat at the Ticino – Q63.
H. French forces cut off in the Lunigiana Mountains – Q76, Q77.
L. French defeat at Vicenza – Q75.
J. French cut off at Turin – Q74.
K. Fall of central Italy; nuclear destruction of Florence and Siena – Q80, Q81.

INVASION OF ITALY

THE END OF THE WORLD

Tu te verras en îles et mers enclos:
Mahommet contraire, plus mer Hadriatique:
Chevaux et d'ânes tu rongeras les os. (III,23)

Naufrage à classe près d'onde Hadriatique:
La terre tremble émue sus l'air en terre mis:
Egypte tremble augment Mahometique,
L'Héraut soi rendre à crier est commis. (II,86)

If, France, your forces pass the sea off north-
west Italy,
You will find yourself trapped between the
islands and at sea.
Mohammed [Arabs] will come against you,
even worse in the Adriatic,
And you will gnaw the bones of horses and
asses in hunger.

The fleet will be wrecked near the Adriatic
Sea.
The earth will be shaken, stirred up, and
thrown into the air.
The forces of Mahommet will be increased in
Egypt,
And the surrendered Announcer will be
ordered to speak.

The conflict has come too close to France to be
ignored any longer, and the French fleet has joined
the war, but will over-extend itself in its initial
enthusiasm, and while attempting to cut the Eastern invaders in Italy off from their Albanian supplies, they will be destroyed in the Adriatic Sea.
Fearing a counter-attack, the Arab forces will

increase their Egyptian defenses. By now, however, they will have gained control of the communications networks throughout the Mediterranean area and will use them for their propaganda warfare.

Q55–Q57. The Easterners Introduce a New Weapon

A Crustamin par mer Hadriatique
Apparaîtra un horrible poisson,
De face humaine, et la fin aquatique,
Qui se prendra dehors de l'hameçon. (III,21)

Durant l'étoile chevelue apparente,
Les trois princes seront faits ennemis:
Frappés du ciel, paix terre tremulente,
Pau. Tymbre undans, serpent sur le bord mis. (II,43)

Quand le poisson terrestre et aquatique,
Par forte vague au gravier sera mis,
Sa former étrange suave et horrifique,
Par mer aux murs bientôt les ennemis. (I,29)

In the River Conca, where it flows into the Adriatic Sea,
There will appear a horrible fish-like creature.
It will have a face like a man, with an aquatic end,
A creature that cannot be captured with a hook.

During the appearance of the bearded star [comet]
When three great powers will be enemies,
The peaceful earth shall quake, struck from the sky,

And where the Po and Tiber overflow [Gulf of
  Venice and Rome], an amphibious creature will
  be put upon the shore.

There will come forth a creature that is both
  terrestrial and aquatic,
It will appear in a strong wave, upon the beach.
Its form will be strange, frightening, but pleasing
  to the eye,
And coming by the sea, it will quickly reach the
  enemies' defenses.

Nostradamus is always pointed in his predictions,
and with the above quatrains he hits three events
simultaneously. He predicts that when Rome and
Venice are attacked, China will be fighting its war
against a US-Russian alliance while Halley's (?)
Comet, scheduled to be seen again in 1986–7, will
be visible in the sky. During the time that this
takes place, the Eastern powers will introduce a
new aquatic weapon, probably a submersible tank,
that with total surprise comes out of the sea and
attacks coastal areas. His description of these weapons resembles pure science fiction. In his mind's
eye he sees them in action attacking the Italian
coast.

Q58. Northern Italy Threatened

Les deux copies aux murs ne pourront joindre,
Dans cet instant trembler Milan, Ticin:
Faim, soif, doutance si fort les viendra poindre
Chair, pain, ni vivres n'auront un seul boucin. (IV,90)

The two forces will be unable to unite on the seas,
And in that instant Milan and Pavia [north Italy]
   will begin to tremble.
Hunger, thirst and doubt will greatly plague them,
For they will not have a single morsel of meat,
   bread or other food to eat.

The destruction of the French [and Italian] fleets
on the high seas and other naval failures will
prevent food reaching the hunger-stricken Italians.
And with the Easterners in control of Venice, the
entire Po Valley will be at their mercy. Inasmuch
as Italy's industry is centered in this area, it will
give them total control. The rule will be so oppres-
sive that it will make the cities "tremble."

Chapter 3

THE CONQUEST OF ITALY

Q59–Q62. The French Counter-offensive in Italy

La gent Gauloise et nation étrange,
Outre les monts, morts, pris et profligés:
Au mois contraire et proche de vendange,
Par les Seigneurs en accord rédigés. (III,38)

Gens d'alentours de Tarn, Loth, et Garonne
Gardez les monts Apennines passer:
Vôtre tombeau près de Rome, et d'Anconne,
Le noir poil crêpe fera trophée dresser. (III,43)

Armée Celtique en Italie vexée
De toutes parts conflit et grande perte:
Romains fuis, ô Gaule repoussée!
Près du Thesin, Rubicon pugne incerte. (II,72)

Près de Tesin les habitants le Loire,
Garonne et Saone, Seine, Tain et Gironde:
Outre les monts dresseront promontoire,

Conflit donné, Pau granci, submergé onde.
  (VI, 79)

Frenchmen and forces from another nation
Will march beyond the mountains to die, to
  be captured or killed.
Near the harvest time [autumn] and in the
  contrary month [January]
By the united Moslim leaders.

People from around the Tarn, Lot and Ga-
  ronne, [French rivers]
Beware of passing the Apennine mountains
  [Italy]!
Your graves will be dug near Rome and
  Ancona [east Italian coast]
The enemy with the frizzled black beard will
  erect a trophy for his victory.

The French army will be vexed in Italy,
And on every side the conflict will cause
  great losses.
The [remaining] Roman forces will flee; the
  French will be repelled
In battles with uncertain outcomes near the
  Ticino and Rubicon rivers.

Those of the Loire will come to the River
  Ticino
As well as those of the Garonne, the Saône,
  the Seine, the Tarn and the Gironde.
They will set up their camp beyond the
  mountains

72

And when the conflict will be ordered, the
 River Po [north Italy] will rise and flood.

The French and the other Western forces operating in the area are not yet ready to admit defeat, and toward the beginning of the new year they will cross the Alps and the Apennine mountains in an attempt to forestall the complete subjugation of all of Italy by the Easterners.

Their attempt will end in utter failure, with major defeats taking place in the area of Rome and on the Adriatic coast. Greatly outnumbered, the remainder of the French and Italian armies will retreat from Ancona in a northward direction toward the River Rubicon near Rimini, and eventually even further until they reach Pavia near the River Ticino.

While at first the outcome of the battles appears to be uncertain, both will end with a total Allied defeat.

Q63. *The French Regroup After Defeat*

Pour la faveur que la cité fera,
Au grand qui tôt perdra champ de bataille,
Fuis de rang Pau, Tessin versera
De sang, feux, morts, noyes de coup de taille.
  (II, 26)

The City of Paris will show favor
To their great leader, but he will soon lose
 the field of battle,

He will take up a position on the River Po,
    after the flooding of the Ticino,
With blood, fires, death, stabbings and drown-
    ings.

The fleeing French army will be in no position to
pose a serious threat to the advancing Easterners,
and a new battle along the Ticino will again result
in another defeat amidst scenes of wanton destruction and death. In order to avoid total annihila-
tion the French commander will withdraw his
battle-weary soldiers in order to regroup on the Po
in the upper valley.

Q64–Q65: *The Sinking of England*

La grande Bretagne comprise d'Angleterre
Viendra par eaux si haut à inonder
La Lique neuve d'Ausonne fera guerre,
Que contre eux ils se viendront bander. (III,70)

Grand Pau, grand mal pour Gaulois recevra,
Vaine terreur au maritime Lion:
Peuple infini par la mer passera,
Sans échapper un quart d'un million. (II,94)

Great Britain, comprising England,
Will be flooded very high with water.
At the same time the League of Ausonia
    [south Italy] will be at war,
And striving against their enemies.

When the French will prepare for great evil at
    the River Po,

THE END OF THE WORLD

The maritime Lion [Britain] will be in hope-
    less terror.
People will flee over the sea in countless
    number,
But a quarter of a million will not escape.

At the very time that the remaining Italian forces
are fighting for their lives and the French are
taking up defensive positions along the River Po
against the Easterners, England will be inundated
to such an extent that her government and people
will be forced to flee the island. This desperate
attempt will cost 250,000 Britains their lives.

It leaves no doubt that Nostradamus predicts in
no uncertain terms the flooding of Great Britain,
but that he limits the destruction to the specific
area "comprising England"—the southern part of
the country. If we take a close look at the map
showing the topographical elevations of Britain, it
can be seen that the portions of land within the
boundaries of England proper are generally lower
than those of its neighbor to the north, Scotland. In three other verses, in fact, Nostradamus
described events to take place on the "Island of
Scotland." Scotland is *not* an island, but it certainly would become one if England were to be
submerged as a result of a major earth disturbance.

Several other seers, both of modern times and
in the past, have made similar predictions con-
cerning Britain:

1) Kentucky prophet Edgar Cayce prophesies
that northern Europe will someday be changed in
'a twinkling of an eye', due to geological alterations;

2) English psychic John Pendragon, who died

in 1970, foresaw London to be partially submerged, and the lowlands of his native nation covered with water;

3) Madame Blavatsky, Oriental mystic and psychic, wrote in 1882 that the British Isles would be the first among many victim-nations to suffer from the earth upheavals and vast floodings;

4) Malthasar Mas, a seventeenth-century psychic prophet, saw in a vision an island overwhelmed by a deluge and swallowed by the sea. Soon after the tragedy Mas claimed to have had a dream in which he saw the waters begin to rise, little by little, and that slowly the upper portions of sunken towers and buildings appeared again.

A voice then told him that what he was witnessing was England reappearing out of the sea.

Q66. London Shaken by a Quake

Le tremblement de terre à Mortara,
Cassich saint George à demi perfondrez,
Paix assoupie la guerre évaillera,
Dans temple à Pâcques abîmes enfondrez. (IX,31)

The earth will tremble at Mortara [north-west Italy]
Tin Saint George [England] half-submerged,
When peace shall sleep and war be awakened,
The temple [Westminster Abbey in London] will rip open with great cracks during Easter.

These verses continue to expand on the destruction of Great Britain, tying the earthquake that will take place at Mortara in north-west Italy together with the tragedy that is being described in the second line, "Tin Saint George half-submerged." Southern England was known to the ancient Phoenicians as the "Tin Island," and Saint George is, of course, England's patron saint. Again, England and not all of Britain is specified to be half-submerged. Is it possible that the trembling of the landmass of Italy will be a sympathetic quake caused by the sudden inundation of a large part of Britain, resulting in a massive shifting of surface weight and pressure?

One unresolved element in Nostradamus's predictive verse is the identification of the "temple" where at Easter great cracks will "rip open" the sanctuary. The verse taken as a whole mentions only two possible locations for the temple; Mortara in Italy, or England. The problem is that there is no temple of any renown in Mortara, but England does possess a temple referred to by Nostradamus on two previous occasions. In the first, known as Century VIII, quatrain 53, the French seer makes mention of a "Temple of the Sun" situated across the English Channel from Boulogne. The British commentator Charles A. Ward identified this temple as Westminster Abbey in London, built upon a former site of a temple to the sun-god Apollo, destroyed in AD 154. The association between the "temple" and Westminster Abbey is further verified in the second verse—Century VI, quatrain 22—where Nostradamus described a "great heavenly temple" situated "at London."

According to the prophecy given above, "In the Temple at Easter 'abysses' will be ripped open." It is interesting that there happens to be a depression along the northern bank of the River Thames which passes beneath the Strand, and Fleet Street and Cornhill in the City of London. If pressure were exerted upon this depression, the bed could easily give way and buckle, not only causing ruptures in the surface of much of London but possibly in the floor of Westminster Abbey in the west.

Q67–Q70. The Eastern Invasion of the West Coast of Italy

Depuis Monech jusque'auprès de Sicille
toute la plage demeurera désolee:
Il n'y aura faubourg, cité ni ville,
Que par Barbares pillée soit et volee. (II,4)

Naples, Palerme, et toute la Sicille,
Par main Barbare sera inhabitée:
Corsique, Salerne et de Sardaigne l'Île,
Faim, peste, guerre, fin de maux intentée. (VII,6)

Classe Gauloise n'approches de Corseigne,
Moins de Sardaigne, tu t'en repentiras:
Trestous mourrez frustrés de l'aide grogne:
Sang nagera: captif ne me croiras. (III,87)

Je pleure Nisse, Mannego, Pize, Gennes,
Sauone, Siena, Capue, Modene, Malte:
Le dessus sang et glaive par étrennes,
Feu trembler terre, eau, malheureuse nolte. (X,60)

From Monaco to Sicily,

THE END OF THE WORLD

The entire coast of Italy will be desolate.
There will not be a single suburb, town or
  city
That will not have been pillaged and robbed
  by the Arabs.

Naples, Palermo and all of Sicily
Will be made uninhabitable at the hands of
  the Arabs.
Also Corsica, Salerno, and the Isle of Sardinia,
Will be affected by famine, disease and war,
  and the end of these evils is not as yet in
  sight.

French fleet, do not approach Corsica!
Much less Sardinia. You will be sorry!
Everyone of you will die frustrated without
  help from land,
You will either swim in your own blood or be
  captured—yet you will not believe me.

I weep for Nice, Monaco, Pisa, Genoa [on
  the Riviera],
Savona, Siena, Modena, [north-west Italy]
  and Malta.
For these there will be a New Year's gift of
  blood and metal;
Fire, the earth will shudder, and floods because
  of unfortunate unwillingness.

Near the first of the year, the Easterners will
start their long-planned massive invasion of the
entire western coast of Italy, the southern part of
France, and the islands of Sicily, Corsica and

Sardinia. Using disease [germ warfare] and "fire which will make the earth shudder" [nuclear weapons] they again will inflict serious losses on the Allies. Whatever has survived of the French fleet after the Battle of the Adriatic will now be overwhelmed and destroyed in and around the islands.

Q71–Q73. The Papacy Forced to Flee to a New Land

Par feu du ciel la cité presque aduste:
L'urne menace encore Deucalion:
Vexee Sardaigne par la Punique fuste,
Après que Libra lairra son Phaeton. (II,81)

Par la puissance des trois roi temporels,
En autre lieu sera mis le saint siège:
Où la substance de l'espirit corporal,
Sera remise et reçus pour vrai siège. (VIII,99)

La grande étoile par sept jours brûlera,
Nuée fera deux soleils apparoit:
Le gros mâtin toute nuit hurlera
Quand grand pontife changera de terroir. (II,41)

Through fire coming down from the sky, the city will be almost totally burned
While at the same time there will be tremendous flooding.
Sardinia will be vexed by the North African fleet
And the Church will have to vacate her seat of power.

THE END OF THE WORLD

By the power of three realms,
The Holy See will be moved elsewhere
Where a new Pope will receive the spirit
And there will be a new Church seat of
  power.

The great star [comet] will burn for seven
  days,
The clouds will cause *two* suns to appear
  [atomic explosion?]
A great dog [?] will howl all night
When the great Pontiff will change countries.

During the appearance of Halley's (?) Comet
(1986–7), when China, Russia and the United
States are at war (Q56), the Papacy will be forced
to leave its traditional capital at Rome and, while
in exile, a new Pope will be elected to enforce the
rule of the Church.

That this forced move of the Seat of Authority
of the Roman Catholic Church will occur amid
violence was revealed to Pope Pius X in a vision
he received in 1909. During an audience with
several people, the Pontiff suddenly fell into a
trance, and emerging from it, he cried out, "What
I see is terrifying! Will it be myself? Will it be my
successor? What is certain is that the Pope will
quit Rome, and in leaving the Vatican he will
have to walk over the dead bodies of his priests"
(see Q45–Q46).

Q74. The French Cut Off in Northern Italy

Sur le sablon par un hideux déluge,
Des autres mers trouvé monstre marin:
Proche du lieu sera fait un refuge,
Tenant Sauone esclave de Turin. (V,88)

A marine creature from foreign seas will be
  discovered,
Coming out of a large wave striking the beach.
It will secure a refuge near the place [of
  landing]
And it shall hold Savona [north-west coast of
  Italy] to make Turin its prisoner.

The Easterners will launch another amphibious
attack using their submersible tanks (Q55–Q57),
and this time their move will be against the north-
west coast of Italy at Savona, near Genoa. From
this beach-head the Easterners will drive toward
Turin. Apparently their aim will be cut off the
French armies positioned in the Po Valley from
their main supply route across the Alps.

Q75–Q77. More French Defeats—The Capture
of Prince Albert

Par le torrent qui descend de Verone
Pars lors qu'au Pau guidera son entrée
Un grand naufrage, et non moins et Garonne,
Quand ceux de Gennes marcheront leur contrée.
  (II,33)

THE END OF THE WORLD

Peuple infini paritra à Vicence,
Sans force, feu brûler la basilique:
Près de Lunage défait grand de Valence,
Lorsque Venise par morte prendra pique. (VIII,11)

Dedans le coin de Luna viendra rendre,
Où sera pris et mis en terre étrange,
Les fruits immurs seront à grand esclandre,
Grand vitupere, à l'un grande louange. (IX,65)

By means of the river that descends from Verona [the River Adige]
They will follow it to where it enters the Po [north Italy].
There will be a great wreck for those of the Garonne [the French].
The enemy near Genoa will march against their country.

Countless people will appear at Vicenza [north-east Italy]
They will come without force, in disarray, and fire will burn the basilica,
Near the Lunigiana valley the heir of Monaco will be defeated
When Venice will die in the war.

He will enter the valley of Lunigiana,
When he will be captured, taken prisoner, and sent to a strange and foreign land.
Unripe fruit will cause a great scandal,
There will be blame, but for him only great praise.

At the same time that Venice will be destroyed (Q50–Q52), and the Easterners land near Savona and Genoa to attack the French positions in northwest Italy (Q74), the French will be defeated in two separate locations. First, the French army will attempt a counter-offensive from Verona, in northeast Italy. They will descend the River Adige toward the mouth of the Po in order to cut Eastern supply lines from the conquered port of Venice. The Eastern victory will be devastating, and the fleeing French will go back up the Adige as far as Vicenza, where the enemy will overtake them and burn the city's cathedral.

A strict translation of the third line of the second quatrain really reads, "Near Lunigiana the great one of Valence defeated." This clearly refers to the man who will be captured in the second battle, in north-central Italy. There the son of Prince Rainier and Grace Kelly—the heir to the throne of Monaco—will find himself and a French army trapped in the central valley of the Lunigiana mountains, and will be captured, and as prisoner taken to the Far East.

In Nostradamus's day, the "great one of Valence" meant the person who held the title Duke of the Valentinois. In 1642 the title was transferred to the Prince of Monaco, and ever since it has been the traditional title of the heir apparent to the throne. The present heir, Prince Albert, is of the right age for military service and will be so through the 1990s.

THE END OF THE WORLD
Q78–Q79. Setbacks for the Easterners

Le conducteur de l'armée Françoise,
Cuidant perdre le principal phalange:
Par sus pavé de l'avoine et d'ardoise,
Soi parfondra par Gennes gent étrange. (VII,39)

Avant qu'à Rome grand aie rendu l'âme,
Affrayeur grande â l'armee étrangère:
Par escadrons l'embuche près de Parme,
Puis les deux rouges ensemble feront chère. (V,22)

The leader of the French army
Will plan to defeat the enemy's principal
    formation
Near a threshing-ground for oats
But the foreign people will undermine their
    own position at Genoa.

Before the great leader dies in Rome,
There will be great terror for the foreign army.
They will be ambushed by squadrons near
    Parma [north Italy]
Then two church leaders will celebrate to-
    gether.

Stubbornly, the French try to regroup their defeated
forces for another offensive, and a tactical error of
the Easterners will make them lose their beach-
head, thereby strengthening the position of the
French. Just before the imprisoned Pope dies
(Q45–Q46) the Eastern forces in the Po Valley
will suffer a significant military setback in the Parma
area, which will cause great optimism among two

church leaders who believe this will be the turning point in the war.

Q80–Q81. *The Easterners Regain Their Losses— Florence under Atomic Attack*

La sainteté trop feinte et seductive,
Accompagné d'une langue diserte:
La cité vieille, et Parme trop hâtive,
Florence et Sienne rendront plus desertes. (VI,48)

Verceil, Milan donra intelligence,
Dedans Ticin sera faite la plaie:
Courir par Seine eau, sang, feu par Florence,
Unique choir d'haut en bas faisant maye. (VIII,7)

By false believing themselves secure and safe,
Through speeches of an eloquent tongue,
The city decays, and Parma will act too prematurely,
Florence and Siena [central Italy] the enemy will turn to desert.

News will come from Vercelli and Milan [north Italy]
Within Pavia a disease will be produced.
It will also be found in the waters of the Seine [Paris]; and blood and fire will be in Florence,
And an important leader will fall while crying for help.

The French-Italian forces will become over-confident because of the first defeats of the Easterners, and this will lead to ill-timed actions. Using nuclear weapons, the Easterners will regain the initiative against Florence and Siena, and will also introduce germ weapons at Pavia. As preparation for the Eastern invasion of France, fifth-columnists will poison the drinking water of Paris with a germ pollutant.

Chapter 4

Assault on France and Spain

Q82–Q83. *The Destruction of Monaco*

De sang et faim plus grande calamité,
Sept fois s'apprête à la marine plage:
Monech de faim, lieu pris, captivité,
Le grand mené croc ferrée cage. (III,10)

La légion dans la marine classe
Calcine, Magnes soufre, et poix brûlera:
Le long repos de l'assurée place;
Port Selyn, Hercle feu les consumera. (IV,23)

Through calamity of blood and famine,
They will come close to shores seven times.
Monaco will die of hunger, the place will be
    captured, [people taken] into captivity
The great leader will be led away in a crunch-
    ing metal vehicle.

The sailors within the marine fleet

Will ignite highly flammable materials
Then there will be a long rest in a secure
  place
And fire will destroy Genoa and Monaco.

There appears to be no way to stop the Easterners'
assault, and they expand their amphibious attacks
in the western Mediterranean to include the coast
of France. Monaco will suffer from famine and
their leader will be captured and led away in an
armored vehicle [half-track?]. Both Monaco and
the city of Genoa which the Easterners lost (Q78)
will be annihilated from the sea with fire.

Q84–Q87. *Sea and Land Attack on the French Riviera*

Dix envoyés, chef de nef mettre à mort,
D'un averti en classe guerra ouverte:
Confusion chef l'un se pique et mord,
Leryns, stecades neft, cap dedans la nerte.
  (VII,37)

Au peuple ingrat faites les remonstrances,
Pars lors l'armée se saisira d'Antibe:
Dans l'arc Monech feront des doleances,
Et à Frejus l'un l'autre prendra ribe. (X,23)

Friens, Antibol, villes antour de Nice,
Seront vastées fort par mer et par terre:
Les sauterelles terres et mer vent propice,
Paris, morts, troussés, pillés sans loi de guerre.
  (III,82)

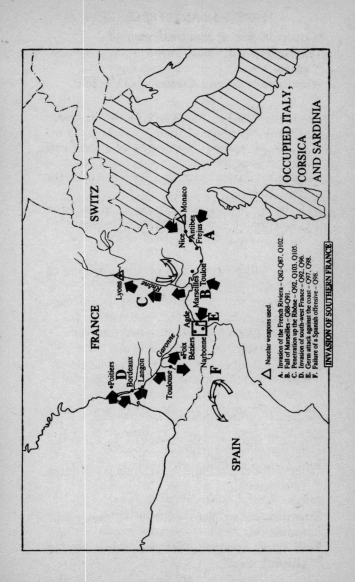

SWITZ

FRANCE

OCCUPIED ITALY,
CORSICA
AND SARDINIA

Lyons

Poitiers

Bordeaux

Langon

Toulouse

Foix

Béziers

Narbonne

Agde

Marseilles

Toulon

Nice

Antibes

Monaco

Frejus

Rhône

Garonne

SPAIN

A
B
C
D
E
F

△ Nuclear weapons used.

A. Invasion of the French Riviera – Q82-Q87, Q102.
B. Fall of Marseilles – Q88-Q91.
C. Penetration up the Rhône – Q92, Q103, Q105.
D. Invasion of south-west France – Q92, Q96.
E. German attack against the coast – Q97, Q98.
F. Failure of a Spanish offensive – Q98.

INVASION OF SOUTHERN FRANCE

Le fort Nicene ne sera combattu:
Vaincu sera par rutilant métal
Son fait sera un long temps débattu,
Aux citadins étrange épouvantal. (VII,19)

Ten assassins will be sent to murder the captain of the ship

He will be warned by another, and the fleets will engage in war.

In the confusion, the two leaders will fight face to face,

At the Lerins Islands [off Antibes] and the Hyer Islands [off Toulon] there will be ships with prows pointed down [sunk].

Threats will be made to a people unwilling to submit,

The army will attack Antibes [south-east France],

This will place Monaco in a bad position,

And at Frejus the shore will be captured.

Frejus, Antibes, towns around Nice [south-east French coast]

Will be thoroughly devastated by sea and by land.

By land and sea will come the locusts, the wind in their favor,

They will capture, kill, bind, pillage, without law of war.

The defenses of Nice will not be engaged in battle,

It will be conquered by an instrument of shining metal.

THE END OF THE WORLD

This event will be remembered for a long
    time,
To the citizens it will be strange and frightful.

As part of their overall planning, the Easterners
will send ten assassins to murder the commander
of the French fleet, but this will be discovered,
and the expected sea battle will take place, with
many ships on both sides going down. The naval
engagement will be part of a coordinated attack to
defeat the French on both land and sea, and the
French cities of Nice, Antibes and Frejus will be
annihilated by Eastern forces that have fanned out
from their initial beach-head at Frejus. It is during
this coordinated effort that the Easterners will
introduce a new weapon into the war; one that
will be strange and terrible and of "shining metal."
It will be so effective that its effect will prevent
the French from using the defenses of Nice.

Q88–Q91. The Battle for Marseilles

La grand Satyre et Tigre d'Hyrcanie,
Don presenté à ceux de l'Océan:
Un chef de classe ira de Carmanie,
Prendre terre au Tyrren Phocean. (III,90)

Par la discorde négligence Gauloise,
Sera passage à Mahammet ouvert:
De sang trempé à la terre et mer Senoise,
Le port Phocen de voiles et nefs couvert. (I,18)

Pieds et cheval à la seconde veille,

Feront entree vastient tout par la mer:
Dedans le poil entrera de Marseille,
Pleurs, cris, et sang, onc nul temps si amer.
  (X,88)

Dedans tonneaux hors oints d'huile et graisse
Seront vingt un devant le port fermés:
Au second guet par mort feront prouesse
Gagner les portes, et du guet assommés. (VII,40)

A great leader known as the Satyr and the
  Tiger of Hyrcania [north Iran]
Will be presented with a gift by those of the
  great Ocean.
A chief of a fleet will set out from Carmania
  [south Iran, on the Persian Gulf]
He will be the one who will invade the shore
  at Tyrean Phocean [port of Marseilles].

Because of disagreement and negligence among
  the French,
A passage will be opened to Mahommet [the
  Arabs].
And at that time the land and seas of Italy
  will be soaked with blood
[While] the Phocean port [Marseilles] will be
  jammed with ships.

A horse's hoof heard at the second watch,
The enemy will force an entry by sea, devas-
  tating everything.
Within the port of Marseilles he will enter,
Tears, cries and blood. Never were times so
  bitter!

Within containers with smooth surfaces
Twenty-one will be closed up outside the
    port.
At the second watch they will be killed in
    their performance,
They will secure an opening and will then be
    felled by the sentries.

The crucial battle for control of the southern coast
of France will be fought at the major French port
of Marseilles. A Far Eastern fleet from the Pacific
will arrive at the Persian Gulf where its command
will be turned over to an Arab leader from the
area of northern Iran. From the Gulf the fleet will
proceed to the western Mediterranean, and attack
Marseilles. The defeat of Italy forces thousands of
people to flee to France and the port of Marseilles
is full of refugee ships. With the defenses of the
port in disorder the Eastern fleet will send twenty
one minisubmarines ashore to establish a "mini-
beach-head." They will succeed in forcing an opening through which the attackers can enter the
port, but the crew of the minisubs will be killed by
the sentries during their mission.

Q92–Q96. *Eastern Penetration into Southern and
South-western France*

*Du tout Marseilles des habitants changée,
Course et poursuite jusque'auprès de Lyon,
Narbonne, Thoulouse par Bordeaux outragé,
Tues captifs presque d'un million.* (I, 72)

Bordeaux, Poitiers, au son de la campane,
A grande classe ira jusqu'a l'Angon,
Contre Gaulois sera leur tramontane,
Quand monstre hideux maîtra près d'Orgon.
  (I,90)

Par la tumeur de Heb, Po, Tag, Timbre, et
  Rosne
Et par l'étang Leman et Aretin,
Les deux grands chefs et cités de Garonne,
Pris, morts, noyés. Partir humain butin. (III,12)

Ruiné aux Volsques de peur si fort terribles,
Leur grande cité teinte, fait pestilent:
Piller Sol, Lune et violer leurs temples:
Et les deux fleuves rougir de sang coulant. (VI,98)

Dans Foix entré Roi ceiulee Turban,
Et regnera moins evolu Saturne:
Roi Turban blanc Bizance coeur ban,
Sol, Mars, Mercure près de la hurne. (IX,73)

There will be a complete change of inhabi-
  tants in Marseilles,
Others will flee and be pursued as far north as
  Lyons.
Narbonne, Toulouse [south-west France] will
  be threatened by the enemy at Bordeaux,
They will kill and capture nearly a million men.

Bordeaux, Poitiers [west France] will hear the
  warning siren,
With a great fleet the enemy will get as far as
  Langon [on the River Garonne]

They will use the north wind against the
French,
And a hideous monster will appear near Orgon
[south-east France].

Because of the activity on the Rivers Ebro
[Spain] Po [Italy], Tagus [Spain], Tiber
[Italy] and Rhône [south-east France],
And near Lake Geneva and Arezzo [Italy]
Two leaders and cities of the River Garonne
Will be taken, murdered, and drowned. The
spoils divided.

Ruin for the Volcae [inhabitants of south-
west France], so very terrible and fearful,
Their great city [Toulouse] stained by a disease-
producing weapon,
When the Sun [Rome] is plundered by the
Moon [Arabs] and their churches desecrated
Two rivers will be reddened with blood.

A leader with a blue helmet will enter Foix
[south-west France],
He will prevail less than a change of Saturn's
appearance [i.e. less than four years],
A leader with a white helmet, an Arab Turk,
his heart will fail him,
With the Sun, Mars and Mercury near Aquarius.

The attack of the Far Eastern fleet on the port of
Marseilles will create havoc in the streets and
those who are able to escape from the massacre
will flee northward toward Lyons. The Eastern

invaders will, although the escapees will be pursued, concentrate their efforts on destroying the stragetic harbor and its defenders and in the process kill and capture nearly a million men. The attack will be gigantic for while Marseilles is being destroyed, the Easterners will also launch a major offensive toward the western coast of France. They will capture Bordeaux, bomb Poitiers, and penetrate up the River Garonne as far as Langon. From there they will proceed by land and the length of the Garonne-Aude Valley, taking the cities of Toulouse, Foix and Narbonne. Using the north wind, they will spread airborne bacteria into the opposing French forces. All this will occur not long after the Eastern destruction of Rome. The fifth quatrain indicates that one of the Arab leaders taking part in the invasion of south-west France will have a military command not lasting more than four years. Another leader will die of a heart attack.

Q97–Q98. Germ Warfare Used in Southern France

Au port de Agde trois fustes entreront,
Portant l'infect, non foi et pestilence:
Passant le pont mil milles embleront,
Et le pont rompre à tierce résistance. (VIII,21)

Deux grands frères seront chassés de'Espagne,
L'aîné vaincu sous les monts Pyrenees:
Rougir met, Rosne, sang Leman d'Alemagne,
Narbon, Blyterre, d'Agath contaminées. (IV,94)

THE END OF THE WORLD

Three ships will enter the port of Agde [south
    French coast]
They will bring an infection, a disease,
Bypassing a bridge they will carry off millions,
But to break the bridge, they will be resisted
    by a third of a million.

Two prominent brothers will come out of
    Spain,
The eldest will be defeated in sight of the
    Pyrenees mountains.
The sea and River Rhône will be reddened
    with blood, as will Lake Geneva and
    Germany,
Narbonne and Béziers will be contaminated
    from Agde.

At the French port of Agde, the Easterners will
release deadly bacteria from three ships specially
equipped for this purpose, and the spreading disease will contaminate the nearby cities of Narbonne and Béziers. From northern Spain two commanders will invade across the Pyrenees in an
attempt to break the Eastern hold on the Garonne-
Aude Valley, but one of the commanders will be
defeated. This move will in no way hinder the
Easterners in their quest for territory, and they
will begin a drive up the River Rhône from Marseilles, meeting stiff resistance at a strategic bridge.
Simultaneously, Eastern airforces will be bombing
Switzerland and Germany.

Q99–Q101. *Eastern Strategy Against Western Europe*

Pau, Verone, Vicence, Sarragousse,
De glaives loin terroirs de sang humides:
Peste si grande viendra à la grande gousse,
Proche secours, et bien loin les remedes. (III, 75)

Le mouvement de sens, coeur, pieds et mains
Seront d'accord. Naples, León, Sicile:
Glaives, feux, eaux: puis aux nobles Romains,
Plongés, tués, morts par cerveau débile. (I, 11)

Sur les rochers sang on verra pleuvoir,
Sol Orient, Saturne Occidental:
Près d'Orgon guerre, à Rome grand mal voir,
Nefs parfondrees, et pris le Tridental. (V, 62)

Pau [France], Verona, Vicenza [Italy], Sargossa
[Spain],
They will be soaked in blood by those from
distant lands.
A very great disease will come to them within
large shells,
Relief through death will be near; remedies
for the living far off.

Logical, physical and emotional action
Will be in coordination. Naples [Italy], León
[Spain] and Sicily
Will be affected by fiery weapons and flood-
ing. At the same time the
Noble Romans will be submerged, killed; dead
because of weak thinking.

THE END OF THE WORLD

Blood will be spurted upon the rocks;
The sun in the east, Saturn in the west.
Near Orgon [south-east France] war; and at
Rome a great evil will be observed.
Ships will sink to the bottom; the rulership of
the seas taken.

The first phase of the Eastern offensive against
Europe will consist of a three-pronged attack against
France, Italy and Spain. There will be extensive
use of nuclear and germ weapons. The agony
wrought by these weapons will be so horrifying
that death will come as a welcome friend, for
there will be no remedies available.

Q102. *The Chinese Attack into France*

L'Oriental sortira de son siège,
Passer les monts Apennins voir la Gaule;
Transpercera le ciel, les eaux et neige,
Et un chacun frappera de sa gaule. (II,29)

The Oriental will leave his seat of power,
And he will pass through the Apennine moun-
tains on his way to France.
He will move through the sky, over seas and
across the mountain snows,
And everyone will be struck with his rod.

The Chinese forces, eager for their share of Europe,
will take part in the assault on France. The same
Oriental leader who attacked southern Russia and
Turkey at the beginning of the war will now travel

further to the west, bringing his forces by air and sea and via the mountains, using his terrible rod-shaped weapon to spread terror and death wherever he goes. (Q30).

Q103–Q104. The Easterners Secure Positions Along the River Rhône

Clarté fulgure à Lyon apparente
Luisant, print Malte, subit sera éteinte:
Sardon, Mauris traitera decevante,
Geneve à Londres à Coq trahison feinte. (VIII,6)

Lorsqu'on verra expiler le saint temple,
Plus grand de Rosne leurs sacrés profaner:
Par eux naître pestilence si ample,
Roi fait injuste ne fera condamner. (VIII,62)

A brilliant flash will be visible at Lyons [southeast France]
Malta will also be taken by a sudden shining weapon; then extinguished.
Mars [war] will treat Sardinia deceitfully.
Swiss exiles will be in London; to the French the appearance of treason.

When the holy temple [St. Peter's in Rome] will be seen plundered,
They who are the greatest power on the Rhône will profane sacred things.
From them will originate a very deadly disease
And a leader will not be condemned for fleeing.

When the Arabs attack Sardinia (Q68, Q69, Q71) and Rome is destroyed by the Eastern assault (Q42–Q46), Eastern forces will take up positions along the Rhône and destroy the city of Lyons with a weapon that will give a brilliant flash. Because of attacks on Switzerland, many of that country's citizens will flee rather than fight; and the French will be suspected of treachery.

Q105. *The Eastern Invasion of East Europe*

Flambeau ardent au ciel soir sera vu
Près de la fin et principe du Rosne:
Famine, glaive: tard le secours pourvu,
La Perse tourne envahir Macedone. (II,96)

A burning light will be seen in the sky at night,
Near the end and the beginning of the River Rhône [at Marseilles and Lyons]
There will be famine, steel weapons; and relief will come too late,
The Middle Easterners will move to invade Macedonia [north of Greece].

The Eastern attacks will be ferocious with burnings and bombings while they move up the Rhône from Marseilles against Lyons. At the same time they will invade the Balkans in an endeavor to cut the Soviet Union off from its Eastern European allies.

Q106. *Attack on the Balkan States*

> *Après la grande affliction du sceptre,*
> *Deux ennemis par eux seront defaits:*
> *Classe d' Affrique aux Pannons viendra naître,*
> *Par mer et terre seront horribles faits.* (V,48)

After a great affliction caused by the Chinese
   "rod,"
Two enemies will be defeated by the attackers.
A fleet from Africa will appear before the
   Pannonians. [Balkan nations]
And by land and sea horrible deeds will take
   place.

While the Chinese are annihilating the Italians
and French with their rod-shaped weapon (Q30–
Q102) a fleet coming from North Africa will enter
the Black Sea and attack Romania, Bulgaria and
south-western Russia.

Q107. *The Chinese-Arab Assault on Southern Spain*

> *De Fez le regne parviendra à ceux d'Europe,*
> *Feu leur cité, et lame tranchera:*
> *Le grand d'Asie terre et mer à grande troupe,*
> *Que bleus, pers, croix à mort dechassera.* (VI,80)

From Fez [north-west Africa] the invaders will
   penetrate further into Europe,
Whose cities will be ablaze, whose inhabitants
   will be murdered.
The great leader of Asia will come by land
   and sea with a great army

In blues and greys they will pursue those of
the cross to death.

The attacks on southern Spain will be a combined
assault carried out by the Chinese and Arab armies
coming from Morocco. They will be identifiable
by their blue and grey uniform [as if they will need
identification!] and as before will use nuclear weapons in their attack. The many references to these
weapons through the Nostradamian predictions must
point to small tactical field explosives, for usage of
the H-bombs as we know them would destroy all
the manpower of all opposing armies in a mere
flash.

Q108–Q113. The Invasion of Spain

La Bisantin faisant oblation,
Après avoir Cordube à soi reprise:
Son chemin long repos pamplation,
Mer passant proie par la Cologna prise. (VIII,51)

De la Felice Arabie contrade,
Naîtra puissant de loi Mahométique:
Vexer l'Espagne, conquester la Grenade,
Et plus par mer à la gent Ligustique. (V,55)

Par les contrées du grand fleuve Bethique,
Loin d'Ibere au Royaume de Grenade
Croix repoussées par gens Mahométiques
Un de Cardube trahira la contrade. (III,20)

France à cinq parts par neglect assaillie,

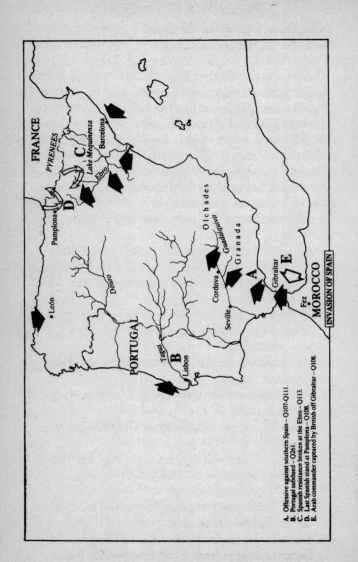

A. Offensive against southern Spain – Q107-Q111.
B. Portugal subdued – Q261.
C. Spanish resistance broken at the Ebro – Q113.
D. Last Spanish stand at Pamplona – Q108.
E. Arab commander captured by British off Gibraltar – Q108.

INVASION OF SPAIN

FRANCE

PYRENEES

Lake Mequinenza

Barcelona

Ebro

Pamplona

León

Douro

Tagus

PORTUGAL

Lisbon

Olchades

Guadalquivir

Cordova

Granada

Seville

Gibraltar

Fez

MOROCCO

A

B

C

D

E

THE END OF THE WORLD

Tunis, Argiels émus par Persiens:
Leon, Seville, Barcelone faillie,
N'aura la classe par les Venetiens. (I,73)

Devant le lac où plus cher fut getté
De sept mois, et son ost déconfit
Seront Hispans par Albanois gastez,
Par délai perte en donnant le conflit. (VIII,94)

Un regne grand demourra désolé,
Auprès de l'Hebro se feront assemblées:
Monts Pyrenees le rendront consolé,
Lorsque dans Mai seront terre tremblées. (VI,88)

The Arab Turk will make an offering to Allah
After having conquered Cordova [south Spain].
His road will lead him to a long rest at
   Pamplona [north Spain]
But while at sea, he will be taken captive by
   those of Gibraltar [British].

In the country of Arabia Felix [south Arabia,
   Yemen]
There will be born one powerful in the ways
   of Mahomet,
He will vex Spain and conquer Granada [south
   Spain]
And by sea he will have fought against the
   Italian people.

Through the great regions of the River Gua-
   dalquivir [south Spain],
Deep into Iberia and Granada,
Christians beaten back by Mahommedan forces

107

A man of Cordova [north of river] will betray
  his country.

France, because of negligence, will be assailed
  in five different areas.
Tunis and Algeria [north Africa] will be
  aroused to fight by the Middle Easterners.
León, Seville, Barcelona [Spanish cities] will
  fall,
And there will be no Allied fleet to offer help.

Near a lake the beloved leader will be put
  down.
For seven months he will resist, but finally
  his army will be routed.
There the Spaniards will be destroyed by the
  Albanians.
They will lose by hesitating to fight.

The Spanish realm will be left desolated.
Near the River Ebro [north Spain] an assem-
  bly for defense will be found.
In May lands will be shaken,
The Pyrenees mountains will console their
  loss.

The Eastern attack against Spain will be led by
two Arab leaders. One will be from Yemen, one
who will already have taken part in the invasion
of Italy; the other will be a Turk who will be
surprised by the British and captured near Gibraltar.
  Forces to be included in the invasion will be
Tunisians and Algerians, together with Albanians,
China's European ally. The Eastern invasion will

begin against southern Spain (Q107) and move across the River Guadalquivir northward. The Easterners' early successes will be partially due to the help of a Spanish leader from Cordova who will betray the Spanish defenses. The cities of Seville, Barcelona and León will be destroyed. Penetrating into northern Spain, however, Eastern forces will meet heavy resistance at two locations. At the River Ebro, which flows through Lake Mequinenza, the Spanish will halt the Eastern advance for seven months. But the death of the Spanish leader will lead to discouragement among the Allied forces and the remaining armies will retreat up the Ebro to make a last stand at Pamplona. Their heroic stand will be of no avail and, after being crushed, the remnants of the army will hide in the Pyrenees mountains during the month of May.

Q114–Q115. Last Allied Resistance in the Mediterranean Crushed

Le chef de Perse remplira grande Olchades,
Classe trirème contre gens Mahométiques
De Parthe, et Mede: et piller les Cyclades:
Repos longtemps au grand port Ionique. (III,64)

Saturne et Mars en Leo Espaigne captive,
Par chef Libyque au conflit attrapé
Proche de Malte, Herodde prise vive,
Et Romain sceptre sera par Coq frappé. (V,14)

When an Arab chieftain from Iran will occupy Olchades [south-east Spain],

A fleet will be formed against the Moham-
medan forces,
The chief will come from Parthia-Media [east
Iran]; the Cyclades island [off Crete] will
be pillaged,
He will rest a long time at the Ionian port
[Syracuse, Sicily].

Saturn and Mars in Leo; Spain captured,
An African chief will lay a trap; conflict.
Near Malta, the Greek navy will be taken
intact
When the Romans will lose the sceptre of
power because of French defeats.

At the time of the Eastern invasion of Spain
(Q75–Q80), an Allied fleet will be assembled in
the Mediterranean to raid Eastern shipping. The
Allied resistance will be effective in destroying
supply bases in the Cyclades and interrupting the
journey of an Arab leader from Iran on the way to
the Spanish front. The Allied fleet, however, will
be defeated near Malta, when the French lose
Italy (Q75–Q77).

Q116. *Easterners Begin Extensive Bombing of Europe*

Planure Ausonne fertile, spacieuse,
Produira taons si tant de sauterelles:
Clarté solaire deviendra nubileuse,
Ronger le tout, grande peste venir d'elles. (IV,48)

The fertile and spacious plain of Ausonia
[Campania, in south central Italy]

THE END OF THE WORLD
Will see many flying creatures and locusts.
The sun will be clouded by their number,
They will destroy everything, and great dis-
ease will originate with them.

Once Italy has fallen, the Easterners will use the
Italian plain of Campania as a major airbase. From
here, Eastern bombers will attack deep into Europe
using their bacterial weapons.

Chapter 5

DEFEAT FOR FRANCE

Q118–Q121. The Fall of Switzerland

Par les Sueves et lieux circonvoisins,
Seront en guerre pour cause des nuées:
Camp marins locustes et cousins,
De Leman fautes seront bien dénuées. (V,85)

Migrez, migrez de Geneve trestous,
Saturne d'or en fer se changera,
Le contre RAYPOZ exterminera tous,
Avant l'avent le ciel signes fera. (IX,44)

Le gros trafic d'un grand Lyon changé,
La plupart tourne en pristine ruine,
Proie aux soldats par pille vendangé:
Par Iura mont et Sueve bruine. (II,83)

Pleurs, cris et plaintes, hurlements, effrayeur,
Coeur inhumain, cruel noir et transi:
Leman, les Îles, de Gennes les majeurs,

Sang épancher, frofaim à nul merci. (VI,81)

Through the Swiss and neighboring lands,
There will be warfare above the clouds.
They will appear as locusts from the sea with
   other flying creatures,
And Geneva will make obvious mistakes.

Leave Geneva, leave everyone of you there.
Saturn [evil] will take your gold in exchange
   for iron.
Zopyra [the deceiver of Babylon] will exter-
   minate all who oppose him,
Before his coming there will be signs in the
   sky.

The large traffic of great Lyons will be blocked.
The greater part of its trade in ruins.
A prey to soldiers, its trade in ruins,
Then they will come through the Jura moun-
   tains and Switzerland in a drizzle.

One will see and hear tears, cries and laments,
   howls of terror,
For they will have inhuman hearts, cruel,
   black and cold,
Who will attack the Mediterranean islands,
   the nobles of Genoa and Lake of Geneva
Blood will be poured out; a famine of wheat,
   and mercy will not be extended.

The neutrality of Switzerland—an attitude which
has kept the country out of war so many times
before—will be of no interest to the Easterners,

and they will attack the mountainous country by air, outmanoeuvring the Swiss army through a tactical error of the Swiss. The city of Geneva will be a specific target of the Easterners in a land attack from northern Italy and south-west France. The Easterners will confiscate the Swiss gold reserves and leave the nation's people impoverished and starving to death. From the information contained in the Nostradamian quatrains it is clear that the attack on Switzerland will occur simultaneously with the Eastern assault on the Italian city of Genoa (Q83), the islands of Sardinia and Corsica (Q68, Q69, Q71), and the destruction of Lyons (Q92, Q103).

Q122. Eastern Thrust into Central France

Tours, Orléans, Blois, Angers, Reims et Nantes,
Cités vexées par subit changement:
Par langues étranges seront tendues tentes,
Fleuves, dards Renes terre et mer tremblement.
(I,20)

Tours, Orleans, Blois, Anger, Reims and Nantes, [east central and north-central France]
Cities that will be vexed by sudden alterations.
Encampments will be pitched by those of foreign tongues,
Floods, darts cast into Rennes [north-east France] trembling of land and sea.

After having secured a beach-head on the south

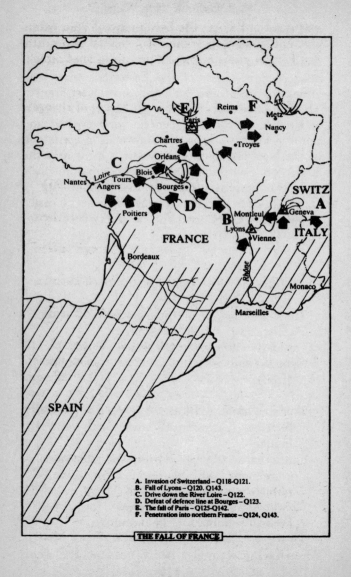

A. Invasion of Switzerland – Q118-Q121.
B. Fall of Lyons – Q120. Q143.
C. Drive down the River Loire – Q122.
D. Defeat of defence line at Bourges – Q123.
E. The fall of Paris – Q125-Q142.
F. Penetration into northern France – Q124, Q143.

THE FALL OF FRANCE

east coast of France, the Easterners will start extensive and saturation bombing of central and northern French cities in preparation for a land attack.

Q123. *Paratroop Defense Line Formed at Bourges*

Les ennemis du fort bien éloignés,
Par chariots conduit le bastion:
Par sur les murs de Bourges égrenés,
Quand Hercules battra l'Haemathion. (IX, 93)

When the enemies are still far from their
    positions,
A defense line will be formed by troops moved
    in by vehicles;
Flying over the crumbling walls of Bourges
    [central France],
An Eastern leader named Hercules will strike.

At the crumbling city of Bourges the French will form a defense line using troops and equipment flown in by air. This will be done well in advance of the expected Eastern attack, led by a man named Hercules, a prominent Eastern commander.

Q124. *Penetration into Northern France*

Le grand conflit qu'on apprête à Nancy,
L'Aemathien dira tout je soumets:
L'Isle Britanne par vin, sel en souci,
Hem. mi. deux Phi. longtemps ne tiendra Mets.
    (X, 7)

A great conflict will be planned against Nancy
    [north-east France]
The Easterner will boast "I will conquer
everything."
The British will be in trouble raising money
    [for defense?]
And the leader Philip will not hold two posi-
    tions at Metz for very long.

There will seem to be no way to stop the Eastern
advances, for they will overrun central France,
and reach as far north as Nancy and Metz, where
they will defeat the armies that have formed two
defense lines, commanded by a military leader
named Philip.

Q125–Q131. Paris Besieged

Gaulois, Ausone bien peu subjeuguera,
Pau, Marne et Seine fera Perse l'vrie:
Qui le grand mur contre eux dressera,
Du moindre au mur le grand perdra la vie.
    (II,63)

Tout à l'entour de la grand cité,
Seront soldats logés par champs et villes:
Donner l'assaut Paris, Rome incité,
Sur le pont lors sera faite grande pille. (V,30)

En cité obsesse aux murs hommes et femmes,
Ennemis hors le chef prêt à soi rendre:
Vent sera fort encontre les gendarmes,

118

THE END OF THE WORLD

Chasés seront par chaux, poussière et cendre.
 (IV,52)

Les fugitifs, feu du ciel sus les piques:
Conflit prochain des corbeaux s'ébattants,
De terre on crie aide, secours celiques,
Quand près des murs seront les combattants.
 (III,7)

De feu volant la machination,
Viendra troubler un grand chef assiégé:
Dedans sera telle sedition,
Qu'en désespoir seront les profligez. (VI,34)

Dans le temple clos le foudre y entrera,
Les citadins dedans leur fort grevés:
Chevaux, boeufs, hommes, l'onde mur touchera,
Par faim, soif, sous les plus faibles armés. (III,6)

Par foudre en l'arche or et argent fondu,
De deux captifs l'un autre mangera:
De la cité le plus grand étendu,
Quand submergée la class nagera. (III,13)

To defend Ausonia [south Italy], the French
 will do poorly.
At the River Po; now at the Rivers Marne
 and Seine [Paris], the Middle Easterners
 will prepare to burn it.
The defender will coordinate a defense against
 them,
But he will die in the weakest point in the
 wall.

All around the great city,
Soldiers will be positioned in field and in
    towns,
Then to assault Paris, near the time Rome is
    aroused,
And upon the Pontificate great pillage car-
    ried out.

In the biggest city, men and women will be
    at the defense line,
And the enemy will be just outside; their
    chief ready to accept surrender.
The wind will blow strongly against their
    forces
And they will be driven back by chemical
    dispersants.

Many fugitives; and fire from the sky will fall
    on pointed weapons.
The conflict is near; flying creatures engage
    in battle.
Below there are cries for relief from above
When the enemy combatants will approach
    the defenses.

The device of flying fire
Will trouble the great chief of the besieged.
Within the city will be dissension and disorder
The leaders will be in despair.

In the closed temple [Notre Dame] a flash of
    lightning will enter,
The citizen defenders within the fort will be
    injured

Men and animals, by the sea forces at the
  defenses,
Affected by famine, even the weakest are
  armed.

Lightning will come through the Arch [of
  Triumph], so hot, gold and silver melted,
Among the prisoners one captive will eat the
  other:
The leader of the city will be stretched out in
  death,
When a submerged fleet will swim toward
  them.

Finally, the French forces who attempted to stop
the Eastern assault in northern Italy along the Po
(Q63 etc.) will find themselves defending their
capital city against the same enemies. This will
occur not long after the destruction of Rome. In
some ways the Eastern attacks can be compared to
the German *Blitzkrieg* of World War II. Eastern
land forces will completely surround Paris, and a
submarine fleet will threaten the city with rocket
and germ weapons. The Parisians will seek Allied
air support but in vain. It appears that in this
battle the Easterners will reveal another one of
their new and unknown weapons; this time one
that will use a beam of destructive light [laser
ray?] that will kill many in the heart of the
city. The commander of Paris's defenses will be
killed, leaving the staunch defenders without a
leader.

121

NOSTRADAMUS PREDICTS
Q132–Q135. *The Surrender of Paris*

La république de la grande cité,
À grand rigeur ne voudra consentir:
Roi sortir hors par trompette cité,
L'echelle au mur, la cité repentir. (III,50)

Du bourg Lareyne parviendront droit à Chartres,
Et feront près de pont Anthoni pause:
Sept pour la paix cauteleux comme Martres,
Feront entrée d'armée à Paris close. (IX,86)

Dans cité entrer exercit déniée,
Duc entrera par persuasion:
Aux faibles portes clam armée amenée,
Mettront feu, mort, de sang effusion. (IX,96)

Par le déluge et pestilence forte,
La cité grande de longtemps assiégée:
La sentinelle et garde de main morte,
Subite prise, mais de nulle outragée. (IX,82)

The republican nation [France] of which the
    great city is the capital,
Will not want to submit to the severe terms
    [of the enemy]:
But the Leader called to battle will leave,
And when the enemy attacks the city's defense
    line, the city will repent.

From Bourg-la-Reine [south of Paris] they will
    travel toward Chartres,
At Pont d'Antony [half-way between] they
    will stop.

Seven [men], crafty, appearing as Martyrs,
  will offer peace,
The route to Paris, closed by an army; the
  enemy will enter it.

The army will be denied entry into the
  city,
The Duke will enter for negotiations:
While at the same time the army will secretly
  penetrate the weakest points in the city's
  defenses
And they begin to destroy it with fire and
  weapons and a great outpouring of blood.

The great city will be besieged for a long
  time
By flood and terrible disease:
The defenders and guards will be killed in
  hand-to-hand combat,
And sudden capture, but none of the civil-
  ians will be harmed.

A French commander will be called to battle somewhere outside Paris and, while he is gone, the
enemy forces will proceed to surround the city. To
avoid wholesale destruction, a peace-team of seven
men will attempt to surrender the city without a
major armed clash, but while negotiations are going
on, both outside the city and within its defense
perimeter, the Eastern forces will find a weak spot
in the Parisian defense lines and will quietly move
into the city after which they will engage in hand-
to-hand combat with its defenders.

Q136–Q138. The Peace of Paris Broken

Les assiégés coloreront leurs paches,
Sept jours après feront cruelle issue:
Dans repoussés, feu, sang Sept mis à l'hache
Dame captive qu'avait la paix tissue. (VII,18)

Des principaux de cité rebellée
Qui tiendront fort pour liberté ravoir:
Detrancher mâles, infelice mêlee,
Cris, hurlements à Nantes piteux voir. (V,33)

Sous un la paix partout sera clamée,
Mais non longtemps pille et rébellion,
Par refus ville, terre et mer entamée,
Mort et captifs le tiers d'un million. (I,92)

Those besieged will feign a peace agreement,
But a week later they will launch a surprise
attack!
They will be forced back inside, amidst fire
and blood; and seven will be executed with
the blade;
And the lady who negotiated the peace will
be held prisoner.

The principal leaders of the city will rebel.
They will strive greatly to recover their liberty.
The men shall be cut up after a disastrous
attack,
And at Nantes, cries and groans and pitiful
sights.

Peace will be proclaimed throughout

But not long after will come pillage and
  destruction.
Because the city will refuse the peace, land
  and sea will be invaded
And there will be one third of a million dead
  and captive men.

With its defenses penetrated and broken down,
the enemy will dictate the capitulation of Paris.
The Parisians will agree but it will only be an
excuse to buy time so that a new attack can be
prepared. After one week's preparation, the French
will break the uneasy truce and attempt a surprise
counter-offensive against the Easterners, but a retaliation of the enemy will force the French resistance fighters to retreat into the city. The seven
male negotiators who dealt with the Easterners
during the surrender negotiations will be rounded
up and executed while the women negotiator of
the surrender team will be jailed. The battle for
Paris as mounted by the resistance forces will result
in the imprisonment and death of no less than
300,000 men.

Q139–Q142. *Paris Destroyed*

L'armée de mer devant cité tiendra,
Puis partira sans faire longue allée:
Citoyens grand proye en terre prendra,
Retourner classe prendre grande emblee. (X,68)

Siège en cité, et de nuit assaillie,
Peu échappé: non loin de mer conflit:

Femme de jois, retour fils defaillie:
Poison et lettres cachées dans le pli. (I,41)

Grand cité à soldats abandonnée,
Onc n'y eut mortel tumulte si proche,
O quelle hideuse calamité s'approche,
Fors une offense n'y sera pardonnée. (VI,96)

La grand cité sera bien désolée,
Des habitants un seul n'y demeurera,
Mur, sexe, temple et vierge violée,
Par fer, feu, peste, canon peuple mourra. (III,84)

The army from the sea will be positioned
before the city,
Then they will leave without making much
of an entrance.
A great many citizens will be held captive in
the surrounding region,
Eventually the fleet will return to seize the
city, and commit great pillage.

The city besieged, will be assaulted at night.
Few will escape—the enemy coming all the
way from the sea,
There will be so few survivors that a woman
will faint to find her son alive.
Poison and letters will be hidden under cover.

The great city will be abandoned by the
soldiers,
Never was a decisive battle fought so near to
it.
The hideous calamity will draw even closer,

And after they will make one counter-attack, nothing will be spared.

The great city will be thoroughly desolated
And of its inhabitants not a single one will remain.
Buildings, churches, women will be violated,
And by bayonet, fire and disease, the people will die.

Without much fanfare, the Eastern armies will once more return to the Eternal City, but this time the campaign will be like a steamroller, overwhelming its defenses and ending with total destruction of both the city and its people.

Q143. The Eastern Thrust into Northern France

Dans Avignon tout le chef de l'empire,
Fera arrêt pour Paris désolé:
Tricast tiendra l'Annibalique ire:
Lyon par change sera mal consolé. (III,93)

At Avignon [south France] the chief of all the conquered lands,
Will make a stop before proceeding to desolated Paris.
Troyes [north-east France] will be occupied by the angry North African,
Lyons [south-east France] will be poorly consoled for its change of inhabitants [army of occupation].

The destruction of Paris will be the signal for the Commander-in-Chief of all the Eastern forces to inspect the conquered lands and he will arrive at Avignon in southern France and travel from there to the ruined city of Paris.

Q144–Q145. A British Attempt to Save Paris

Longtemps sera sans être habitée,
Où Signe et Marne autour vient arroser:
De la Tamise et martiaux tentée,
Déçus les gardes en cuidant repousser. (VI,43)

Le grand secours venu de la Guyenne,
S'arrêtera tout auprès de Poictiers:
Lyon rendu par Mont Luel et Vienne,
Et saccagés partout gens de metiers. (XII,24 add.)

For a long time it [the city] will remain uninhabited,
Where the Rivers Seine and Marne flow together [Paris].
Warriors of the Thames [the British] will try to reach them,
The defenders deceived in trusting the offensive.

A great relief will come from Guienne [south-west France],
But it will be halted near Poitiers [west France].
Lyons [south-east France] surrendered through Montleul and Vienne [east and south of the city],

THE END OF THE WORLD

And people hoarding goods will be robbed.

The Eastern forces have succeeded in destroying the city of Paris, but not before the Western Allies have attempted to save it. A British taskforce will land in south-west France and stab on through to the capital, but will be stopped at Poitiers. The city's defenders will believe themselves saved and will trust in the power of the British army, but it will be in vain. This attempt at salvaging the city will take place around the same time that Lyons is overrun by the enemy. (Q92, Q103, Q120, Q143).

Chapter 6

THE LAST RESISTANCE—
THE FALL OF EUROPE

Q146–Q149. *The British Landing in South-west*
France

Euge, Temins, Gironde et la Rochelle:
O sang Troien! Mars au port de la flèche:
Derrière le fleuve au fort mise à l'échelle,
Pointes à feu grand meurte sur la brèche. (II,61)

Du plus profond de l'Occident Anglois
Où est le chef de l'Île Britannique,
Entrera classe dans Gyronde par Blois,
Par vin et sel, feux cachés aux barriques. (V,34)

Vers Aquitaine par insult Britanniques
De par eux-mêmes grandes incursions.
Pluies, gelées feront terroirs uniques,
Port Selyn fortes fera invasions. (II,1)

Par cité franche de la grande mer Seline,
Qui porte encore à l'estomac la pierre,

Angloise classe viendra sous la bruine
Un rameau prendre, du grand ouverts guerre.
  (V,35)

Bravo, those of the Thames [the British],
  occupying Gironde and La Rochelle [south-
  west French coast].
Oh French blood! War will come to Toulon
  [south-west France].
On the river [the Garonne] the city will be
  assaulted
With pointed weapons with fire; great murder
  at the breakthrough.

From the most secure area of England-of-the-
  West [Canada?]
Where the government of the British Isles
  will be,
Their fleet will enter the Gironde by means
  of capturing Blaye [south-west France]
Through raised money they will purchase hid-
  den fires in containers.

Toward Aquitaine [south-west France] will
  come those of the British Isles,
Alone, they will make an important invasion.
Rain and frost will make the soil difficult to
  move on,
The enemy will use the port of Genoa as an
  important base.

To the leading French city on the Bay of
  Biscay [Bordeaux],
With its rocky coastline,

The English fleet will come amid drizzly
   weather,
To establish a beach-head; and war will be
   declared by the great leader.

It now appears that after the terrible flooding and
subsequent evacuation of the British Isles, the
British will reorganize themselves in Canada to
begin the planning for the reconquest of Europe.
From Hudson Bay, a British invasion force will
leave to establish a beach-head on the south-west
coast of France. Although the weather compli-
cates the landing, the British gunfire and nuclear
weapons will enable them to move inland via
their beach-head at Gironde [the mouth of the
River Garonne], take Bordeaux, and continue their
drive toward Toulouse.

Q150–Q154. The English Offensive Along the Garonne-Aude

L'entrée de Blaye par Rochelle et l'Anglois
Passera outre le grand Aemathion:
Non loin d'Agen attendra la Gaulois,
Secours Narbonne déçu par entretien. (IX,38)

La cité prise par tromperie et fraude,
Par le moyen d'un beau jeune attrapé:
Assault donné Raubine près de L'Aude,
Lui et tous morts pour avoir vien trompé. (III,85)

L'Aemathion passer monts Pyrénées,
En Mars Narbon ne fera résistance:

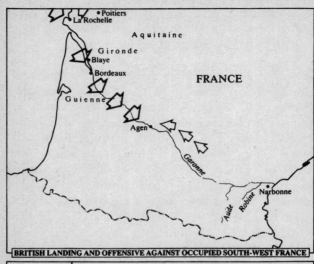

BRITISH LANDING AND OFFENSIVE AGAINST OCCUPIED SOUTH-WEST FRANCE

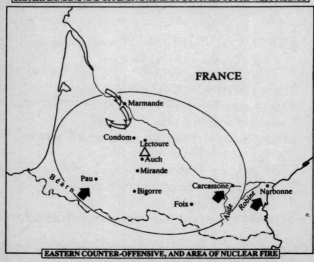

EASTERN COUNTER-OFFENSIVE, AND AREA OF NUCLEAR FIRE

THE END OF THE WORLD

Par mer et terra fera si grand menée,
Cap. n'yant terre sûre pour demeurance. (IX,64)

Bien contigue des grands monts Pyrénées,
Un contre l'Aigle grande copie addresser:
Ouvertes veines, forces exterminees,
Que jusqu'a Pau le chef viendra chasser. (IV,70)

Proche del duero par mer Tyrrene close.
Viendra percer les grands monts Pyrénées,
La main plus courte et sa perce close,
À Carcassonne conduira ses menées. (III,62)

In Nostradamus's scenario of World War III, it appears that the British Expeditionary Force is ready to commit everything in order to stop the Eastern advance, and these quatrains show the beginning of what could be a successful counter-offensive.

The English will enter Blaye and La Rochelle [south-west French coast],
Those who occupy Macedonia [the Easterners] will withdraw.
Not far from Agen [on the River Garonne] the French forces will wait,
The help of Narbonne [south French coast] persuaded by negotiation.

The city secured by persuasive agreement [Narbonne],
Will suddenly be captured again, by means of a youthful enemy leader.

135

When others will counter-attack along the
  Rivers Robine and Aude,
They and their leaders will be killed: having
  been deceived.

The occupants of Macedonia [the Easterners]
  will attack across the Pyrenees,
Narbonne will not offer resistance.
The secret plans of the enemy will be carried
  out on land and sea,
The French will have little land of their own
  to live on.

Quite close to the Pyrenees mountains,
One will command a great army against the
  forces of the Eagle [USA]:
Blood veins will be opened; forces will be
  exterminated,
And as far as Pau [south France] will he chase
  the chief.

By way of the River Duero [north Spain] and
  the closed western Mediterranean,
One will come to pierce across the Pyrenees
  mountains.
He will have one hand shorter than the other,
  and hold a glowing rod.
He will make his [battle] plans at Carcassone.

The British invasion of south-west France will be
part of a plan to cut Eastern-occupied Spain off
from France, along the Garonne-Aude valley, as
well as to gain an opening into the blockaded
Mediterranean. For this plan to have any degree

of success at all, the British at the western end of
the valley will have to link up with the French
resistance forces fighting in the center of the valley at Agen, after which the combined forces are
to move on to Narbonne on the Mediterranean
coast. The resistance fighters in Narbonne are in
agreement with the plan but a sudden attack from
the Easterners from a base in northern Spain will
force a change in plans. A Chinese commander
with a deformed hand will unleash the destructive
power of his glowing rod-shaped weapon (Q30,
Q102), and will establish his new command post
at Carcassone. As a result of sudden action, the
British and accompanying American forces will be
slaughtered along the Rivers Aude and Robine in
the center of the valley. It was a daring move for
the Allied forces, but one that was practically
doomed from the very beginning for by this time
the Easterners control almost all of France.

*Q155–Q160. The Offensive Halted by Nuclear
Weapons*

À quarante-huit degré climatérique,
À fin de Cancer si grande secheresse:
Poisson en mer, fleuve, lac cuit hectique,
Bearn, Bigorre par feu ciel en détresse. (V,98)

Condom et Aux et autour Mirande,
Je vois du ciel feu qui les environne:
Sol Mars conjoint au Lion, puis Marmande
Foudre, grande grêle, mur tombe dans Garonne.
   (VIII,2)

Tout auprès d'Aux, de Lecture et Mirande
Grand feu du ciel en trois nuits tombera:
Cause aviendra bien stupende et mirande:
Bien peu après la terre tremblera. (I,46)

Le boute-feu par son feu attrapé,
De feu du ciel à Cartas et Cominge:
Foix, Aux, Mazere, haut viellard échappé,
Par ceux de Hasse, des Saxons et Turinge.
  (V,100)

Le né difforme par horreur suffoqué,
Dans la cité du grand Roi habitable:
L'édit sévère des captifs revoqué,
Grêle et tonnerre, Condom inestimable. (V,97)

Avant conflit le grand mur tombera,
Le grand à mort, mort trop subite et plainte,
Né imparfait: la plupart nagera:
Auprès de fleuve de sang la terre teinte. (II,57)

From the forty-eight degree [from the north],
At the end of Cancer [June 21] will be a very
  great drought.
Fish in the rivers, lakes and at sea will be
  boiled,
Bearn and Bigorre [south-west France] in dis-
  tress, because of fire from the sky.

At Condom and Auch, and around Mar-
  mande,
I see fire from the sky encompassing them.
Sun and Mars in Leo, also at Mirande

Will fall lightning and great hail. Walls crumbling into the River Garonne.

Very near Auch, Lectoure and Mirande [southwest France]
A great fire will descend from the sky for three days and nights.
It will be considered a stupendous and marvelous event
Causing the earth to shudder.

The one who created the conflagration will be trapped in his own fire,
The fire from the sky will reach Carcassone and Comminges,
Foix and Auch. A prominent elderly statesman will escape
Through the help of Germans.

The one born deformed [the short-handed Chinese leader] will be suffocated in horror
In the city once inhabited by kings [Carcassone].
The severest command against the treatment of captives will be revoked,
Hail and thunder will come down at Condom [south-west France]; damage inestimable.

Before the conflict when the great wall [in the Far East?] will fall,
A great leader will die—a death too sudden. It will be lamentable.
He who will be born imperfect, when many will die in the water

Near a river [Garonne], the land is stained
with blood.

In order to halt the British onslaught in France,
the Chinese leader with the deformed hand (Q154)
will detonate a series of high-altitude, high-yield
atomic devices. The resulting heat will ignite the
atmosphere and the ionized gases will fall as fire.
An extensive area of south-west France will be
burned in the terrible conflagration.

The Chinese leader who ordered this costly attack
has, however, made a serious miscalculation that
will end by costing him his life. The nuclear fire
will reach his command post at Carcassone (Q154),
and he and his forces will be suffocated by the
scorching heat. The atomic fire will also cause
severe weather throughout the affected area. One
leader, important to the Western cause, will die a
sudden death but another will manage to escape
the Holocaust with the aid of German forces.

Q161–Q165. The "Island of Scotland" invaded

Le chef de Londres par règne l'Americh,
L'Îsle d'Escosse tempiera par gelée,
Roi Reb auront un si faux Antechrist,
Que les mettra trestous dans la mêlée. (X,66)

Dedans les Îles si horrible tumulte,
Rien on n'ouira qu'une bellique brigue,
Tant grand sera des prédateurs l'insulte
Qu'on se viendra ranger à la grande ligue.
  (II,100)

THE END OF THE WORLD

Sous le terroir du rond globe lunaire,
Lors que sera dominateur Mercure:
L'Îsle d'Escosse fera un luminaire,
Qui les Anglois mettra à déconfiture. (V,93)

La bande faible le terre occupera,
Ceux du haut lieu feront horrible cris:
Le gros troupeau d'estre coin troublera,
Tombe près Dinebro découverts les escris. (VIII,56)

Le chef d'Escosse, avec six d'Allemagne
Pars gens de mer Orientaux captif:
Traverseront le Calpre et Espagne,
Present en Perse au nouveau Roi craintif. (III,78)

The chief of London will reside in America
[continent],
The Island of Scotland will suffer from frost.
The King and the Rebel will be confronted
by a non-Christian force [Muslims],
His presence will place them in conflict with
each other.

Within the British Isles there will be a horrible uproar,
Only the faction demanding war will be
allowed to be heard.
They will come as plunderers, and so great an
insult,
That others will want to join in the great
league of the conquered.

By means of those of the Moon [Arabs]
When Mercury will be dominating the sky,

The Island of Scotland will have a knowledgeable leader,
One who will put the English into confusion.

A weak force will occupy the land,
Those hiding in the hills will utter horrible
cries against them.
The largest number of the forces near the
coast, suddenly troubled
By discovery. Their cries and defeat near
Edinburgh.

The chief of Scotland, with six prisoners from
Germany,
Will be taken captive by Oriental seamen.
They will pass by Spain, through Gibraltar,
To be presented to a fearful new leader in
Iran.

The defeat of the British forces in France is by no
means the end of trouble for the British. The
sinking of England forces the government to move
to North America, leaving Scotland as an island.
With the Easterners controlling western Europe,
the British will seek to use their only remaining
bastion, Scotland, as a military base. The Scots,
however, will object, and an agitator will arise to
defy the British rights of sovereignty over the
"island." The exiled government will send an expeditionary force to occupy Scotland, forcing the
rebel leader to seek refuge in the hills.

Instead of decreasing tension, the British occupation force will increase the problems besetting

the "island" and some of the rebelling Scots will secretly seek aid from the Easterners. This treasonable action will have the desired results for, sure of the aid ot the subversive elements within the country, the Easterners will finally attack, first defeating the British coastal defenses, later on the main force near Edinburgh. The crowning feat of their victory will be the capture of the British commander, who, with six German prisoners, will be sent to Iran by way of Gibraltar.

Q166–Q169. The Fall of Fortress London

La grand cité d'Ocean maritime,
Environnée de marais en cristal:
Dans le solstice hyemal et la prime,
Sera tentée de vent espouvantal. (IX,48)

Un peu devant que le Soleil s'esconse,
Conflit donné grand peuple dubieux:
Profligés, port marin ne fait reponse,
Pont et sépulcre en deux étranges lieux. (I,37)

La fortresse auprès de la Tamise
Cherra par lors le Roi dedans serré:
Auprès du pont sera vu en chemise
Un devant mort, puis dans le fort barré. (VIII,37)

Les bien aisés subit seront démis,
Par les trois frères le monde mis en trouble,
Cité marine saisiront ennemis,
Faim, feu, sang, peste et de tous maux le double.
    (VIII,17)

The great city of the maritime Ocean [London]
Will be surrounded by a flood of shallow water,
    covered with ice.
In December and in the spring,
It will suffer from hurricane winds.

Shortly before the setting of the sun,
The battle-cry will be sounded, and a great
    people will be left in doubt:
Destroyed, the marine port [of London] will
    be silent
And a bridge and graves will be uprooted.

The fortress near the Thames [London],
Will fall when its Leader will be besieged
    within.
Near the bridge he will be seen in his shirt,
And will confront death when trapped in the
    fort.

Those who thought themselves secure, will
    be suddenly destroyed.
Through three powers at war the world is in
    trouble.
The enemy will seize the marine city [London]
And its inhabitants will suffer from famine,
    fire, flooding, disease and every evil will be
    multiplied.

The flooding of England will leave parts of London intact although it will have the appearance of
a city-island. The shallow waters surrounding the
metropolis will freeze over during the winter sea-

son and the city will constantly be exposed to relentless storms.

One evening, shortly before sunset, the Easterners will surround the city-island and fire and disease will spread over the remains of England, and the city will become devoid of all life.

Q170–Q171. A New Threat in Northern Europe

Persécutée sera de Dieu l'Église,
Et les saints Temples seront expoliés,
L'enfant la mère mettra nue en chemise,
Seront Arabes aux Polons ralliés. (V,73)

Faibles galères seront unies ensemble,
Ennemies faux le plus fort en rempart:
Faibles assailies Vratislaue tremble,
Lubecq et Mysne tiendront barbare part.
  (IX,94)

The Church of God will be persecuted,
And the Holy Temple will be plundered.
A child will turn against its provider,
The Arabs will find an ally in the Poles!

Weak navies will be united,
But secretly, the enemies will penetrate the
    strong defenses.
When the weak navies will be attacked,
    Bratislava [Austria, Czechoslovakia and
    Hungary] will tremble,
Lubeck and Meissen [East Germany] will ally
    with the Arabs.

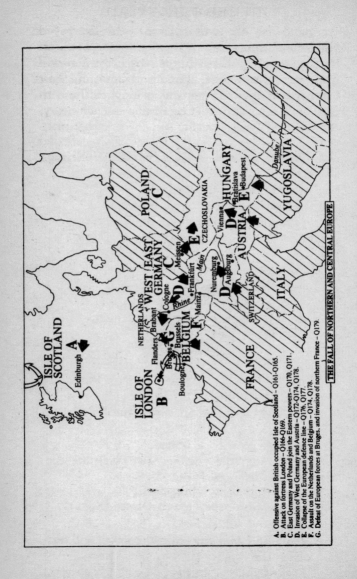

THE FALL OF NORTHERN AND CENTRAL EUROPE

A. Offensive against British occupied Isle of Scotland – O161-O165.
B. Attack on fortress London – O166-O169.
C. East Germany and Poland join the Eastern powers – O170, O171.
D. Invasion of West Germany and Austria – O172-O174, O178.
E. Collapse of the European defence line – O176, O177.
F. Assault on the Netherlands and Belgium – O174, O178.
G. Defeat of European forces at Bruges, and invasion of northern France – O179.

At the same time that Rome was destroyed
(Q42–Q46) the Allies' resistance in the Mediterranean stopped (Q114–Q115), the Easterners will
find sympathizers and allies in Poland and East
Germany. This will be a serious blow to the central European nations—Czechoslovakia, Hungary,
Austria and West Germany—in their defense planning. Even the navies of some of the smaller
countries will not be able to halt the Easterners'
advancing forces.

Q172–Q174. The Invasion of West Germany and Austria

La grand ruine des sacrés ne s'éloigne,
Prouence, Naples, Sicille, Seez, et Ponce,
En Germanie, au Rhin et la Cologne,
Vexés à mort par tous ceux de Magonce. (V,43)

Quand le plus grand emportera le prix,
De Nurenberg, d'Ausbourg, et ceux de Basle,
Par Agrippine chef Frankfort repris
Traverseront par Flamant jusqu'en Gale.
*   (III,53)*

La saint Empire viendra en Germanie,
Ismaelites trouveront lieux ouverts:
Ânes voudront aussi la Carmanie,
Les soutenants de terre tous couverts. (X,31)

A great ruination and destruction is not far
   off,

When it will be in Provence [south France],
    Naples [Italy], Sicily and to the Holy See
    and Pontiff,
Then it will [also] come to Germany, aimed
    against the River Rhine at Cologne
By forces coming from the direction of Mainz.

Once a leader will win the prize,
Of Nuremburg, Augsburg [south Germany]
    and those of Basle [Switzerland]
Through Cologne; the chiefs of Frankfort taken
They will march through Flanders [the Low-
    lands; Netherlands and northern Belgium]
    into France.

He will march into Germany and Austria
The Arabs will find openings in the defenses.
At the same time destruction will come to
    Carmania [south Iran]
The defenders will be buried in the earth.

In moves reminiscent of events of World War II, armies will maneuver over Europe like the pawns in a wild game of chess. As if their supplies are inexhaustible, the Easterners will attack West Germany and Austria as soon as they have strengthened their rule over Italy and southern France. One attack on West Germany will come from East Germany and move down the River Main to Mainz, cutting the nation east-west, and north-south on the Rhine. From Mainz, forces will attack northward toward Cologne, and at Frankfurt Eastern forces will capture the commander of the West German armies.

A second Eastern force will originate from Switzerland and catapult itself into southern West Germany, capturing Nuremburg, and Augsburg.

Eventually the Easterners will extend their invasions into the Netherlands, Belgium and northern France. There is, however, a ray of hope, for while these battles for Western Europe are taking place, Western forces are striking at the heart of the Middle East. They will make a daring raid in the Persian Gulf; a major naval station for Eastern naval forces. (Q88).

Q175. The Death of a German Commander

Auprès du Rhin des montagnes Noriques,
Naîtra un grand de gens trop tard venu,
Qui deféndra Saurome et Pannoniques,
Qu'on ne saura qu'il sera devenu. (III,58)

Near the River Rhine, from the Noric [Austrian] mountains,
Will come a great leader, but he will arrive too late.
He will plan a defense line through central Europe to south-west Russia,
But his destruction will be so complete, that they will be unable to find him.

In an attempt to contain the Eastern forces, an Austrian general will hastily build a defense line running all the way from Austria to the Soviet Union. His aim at keeping the Easterners in southern Europe from uniting with their counterparts in

Poland/East Germany will run into deep trouble. His plans will be discovered and his armies destroyed. His failure will be so total that even his body will never be found.

Q176. A Second German Commander—A Traitor

Un capitaine de la grand Germanie,
Se viendra rendre par simulé secours
Au Roi des Rois aide de Pannonie,
Que sa révolte fera de sang grand cours. (IX,90)

A captain or greater German [West Germany]
Will secretly aid the enemy
To the Eastern leaders he will betray the
  Balkan defenses
And his treason will cause a great flow of
  blood.

Another German commander will help bring about the downfall of the Central European defenses by betraying its plans to the Easterners. A blood bath will be the result.

Q177. The Fall of the Central European Defenses

Près de Sorbin pour assaillir Ongrie,
L'héraut de Brudes les viendra avertir:
Chef Bizantin, Sallon de Sclauonie,
À loi d'Arabes les viendra convertir. (X,62)

THE END OF THE WORLD

From Sorbic Saxony [East Germany] a force
    will assail Czechoslovakia and Hungary,
The announcer at Budapest will sound the
    alarm.
The Arab chief will attack from central and
    northern Yugoslavia,
And will convert them to the ways of the
    Arabs.

The fall of the Central European defense line as
mentioned above (Q176) will be due to a simulta-
neous attack by Eastern forces from East Germany
and Yugoslavia, aided by the German traitor, and
after this there will be little left of Europe that can
be called 'free'.

Q178. Eastern Assault on Holland and Belgium

Translatera en la grande Germanie,
Brabant et Flandres, Gand, Bruges et Boulogne:
La trêve feinte, le grand Duc d'Armenie
Assaillira Vienne et la Cologne. (V,94)

After marching into great Germany [West
    Germany]
They will march against Brabant [Netherlands],
    Flanders, Ghent and Bruges [Belgium] and
    Boulogne [north France]
And after bluffing peace, the Eastern Duke
Will attack Vienna and Cologne.

After the downfall of West Germany and Austria
(Q174), the Easterners will use the West German

151

facilities and use the country as a staging area for an attack on the Netherlands, Belgium and northern France (Q173).

Q179. *The Last Stand by the Allies in Europe—at Bruges*

Saturn au boeuf joue en l'eau, Mars en flèche,
Six de Février mortalité donnera,
Ceux de Tardaigne à Bruges si grande brèche,
Où à Ponteroso chef Barbarin mourra. (VII,49)

With Saturn in Taurus, Jupiter in Aquarius,
   Mars in Sagittarius,
February the 6th will see death.
Those of Tardaigne [north France] at Bruges
   [north-west Belgium] will cause such a set-
   back,
That the Arab will die on a red bridge.

The sad moment has finally arrived. The last Western force in Europe will be forced to make their final stand in Bruges, in Belgium, the country where Napoleon once made *his* last heroic effort to survive. The tired and worn-out Europeans will be no match for the overwhelming flood of Eastern might and firepower and the battle will end with a Western defeat. The killing of an important Eastern general is but a small victory.

   With the fall of Bruges (Q178) and the Eastern thrust into northern France, practically all of the European continent will be controlled by the armies from the Far East and the Middle East—and their unquenchable thirst for land has finally been brought to a halt.

There is simply nowhere else to go.

Chapter 7

TURNING POINT—THE USA AND RUSSIA TAKE THE OFFENSIVE

Q180. *Several Nuclear Attacks Against the United States*

L'aîné vaillant de la fille du Roi,
Repoussera si profond les Celtiques,
Qu'il mettra foudres, combien en tel arroi,
Peu et loin, puis profond ès Hesperiques. (IV,99)

The brave son of the army leader's daughter,
Will defeat the forces of the French.
He will also launch thunderbolts, at first many,
   and targeted,
Then few and at random, deep into the
   Hesperias [the Americas].

With the war in Europe practically won by the Arab and Chinese hordes, the attention of the conquerors will now be directed toward the Americas; hoping to capture the Eagle as well. The grandson of a prominent Chinese leader will play a major role, not only in the conquest of France, but also in directing the Eastern might against the Americas. The first strikes will be large in number and aimed at specific strategic targets, after which the bombing will be intermittent and without being directed at pre-selected sites.

Q181. Mass Destruction Among the Northern Powers

Les lieux peuplés seront inhabitables:
Pour champs avoir grande division:
Regnes livrés à prudents incapables:
Lors les grand frères mort et dissension. (II,95)

The populated places will be made uninhabitable,
Great discords to obtain food from the fields,
Lands will be governed by incapable officials,
And among the great brothers [the United States and Russia] chaos and death.

The nuclear bombardment and radiation, affecting both Russia and the United States, will force entire cities to be evacuated. Food, otherwise so abundant, will suddenly become in short supply, probably because of radiation and germ warfare. Governments at both local and national levels will be unable to meet the crisis and chaos and death will be the order of the day.

Q181a. Economic Chaos in the United States

Mis trésor temple, citadins Hesperiques,

THE END OF THE WORLD

Dans icelui retiré en secret lieu:
Le temple ouvrir les liens fame liques,
Rapris, ravis, proie horrible au millieu. (X,81)

The temple where Hisperian [American] citizens will place their treasures,
That which is stored in a secret place:
The hungry and starving will break the bonds to open the temple,
Treasure will be re-taken, the temple ravaged, a horrible riot in their midst.

The government will no longer be able to control the dissidents and rioters that roam the streets. Hungry and diseased, suffering from radiation and poison, they have no reason to fear anything, and in their quest for money with which to buy the meagre supplies still available, rioters will storm the banks which had been closed because of the economic depression. There will be no way to ward them off, and pitched battles will be fought among the citizens for the possession of the stolen treasure.

Q182. Nuclear Fire Burns New York City

Cinq et quarante degrés ciel brulera,
Feu approcher de la grande cité neuve:
Instant grande flamme éparse sautera,
Quand on voudra des Normans faire preuve. (VI,97)

The sky will appear to burn from the forty-fifth parallel;

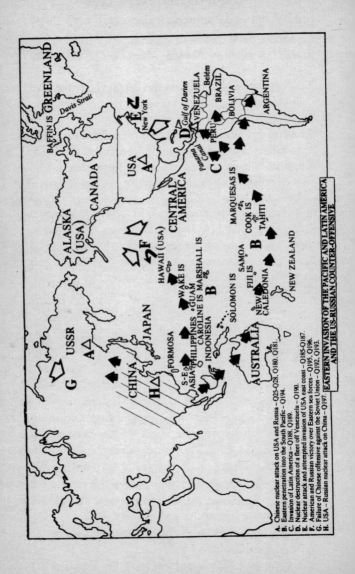

A. Chinese nuclear attack on USA and Russia – Q25-Q28, Q180, Q181.
B. Eastern penetration into the South Pacific – Q194.
C. Invasion of Latin America – Q188, Q189.
D. Nuclear destruction of a fleet off Venezuela – Q190.
E. Nuclear attack and attempted invasion of USA east coast – Q185-Q187.
F. American and Russian victory over Eastern sea forces – Q195, Q196.
G. Failure of Chinese offensive against the Soviet Union – Q192, Q193.
H. USA – Russian nuclear attack on China – Q197. **EASTERN INVASION OF THE PACIFIC AND LATIN AMERICA AND THE US-RUSSIAN COUNTER-OFFENSIVE**

The fire will approach the great city [New York City]:

In an instant a great scattered flame will leap up,

When the French will be tested to the fullest.

A CONFLAG system [Cluster Orbital Nuclear Fire-Weapon for Light Atmosphere Ignition], launched from China, will be detonated above New England [USA], and will create a fire in the upper atmosphere that will reach as far south as New York City. This will occur during the time when France is fighting for its very existence.

The modern California psychic Criswell also has predicted that in the 1980s a foreign power will bomb the United States with nuclear missiles. He predicts that many will be destroyed by anti-missile defenses, but that others will indeed get through the US defenses and land on strategic targets. He specifies that the State of Vermont will be severely affected by a nuclear Holocaust. It is interesting that the fourth parallel of which Nostradamus speaks, and which he claims will be the point where the fire will originate that will burn New York, is the border line between the American State of Vermont and Canada. If a cluster of nuclear devices were detonated simultaneously at a high altitude above Vermont, the resulting firestorm would burn out all of New England—including New York City.

Q183–Q184. *New York Shaken by an Earthquake*

Ennosigée feu du centre de terre,
Fera trembler autour de cité neuve,
Deux grands rochers longtemps feront la guerre,
Puis Arethuse rougira nouveau fleuve. (I,87)

Jardin du monde auprès de cité neuve,
Dans le chemin des montagnes cavées,
Sera saisi et plongé dans la Cuve,
Buvant par force eaux soufre envenimées.
  (X,49)

Volcanic fire from the center of the earth,
Will cause an earthquake around the new city
  [New York City]
Two great rocks will oppose one another for a
  long time,
Then rivers will turn red.

Garden of the world near the new city,
On the way to the man-made mountains [sky-
  scrapers?],
They will also be taken and plunged into the
  bay,
Its people forced to drink poisoned stinking
  water.

Whether it will happen around the same time as
the fire-storm emanating from the forty-fifth parallel or not is an open question, but these quatrains
refer to a catastrophe that could well be triggered
by earth tremors set off by atomic blasts. It bluntly
predicts that New York City and its environs will

be partially destroyed by an earthquake. The force of the quake will be so great in some areas that many of Manhattan's sky-scrapers will be toppled into New York harbor. Water mains will be broken, and the remaining drinking water will be heavily polluted.

In his prediction of the destruction of New York City, Nostradamus was far ahead of his present-day colleagues who forecast a very similar event. Many of them have made predictions in recent years in which they agree with the seer that something ominous is brewing in the rock strata underlying the great island's metropolis.

California's Criswell predicts a sinking of New York in the 1980s. Earth tremors, he says, will reshape the east coast of the United States. He claims that Long Island will be submerged, and soon after Manhattan will become the "Venice of America"—a city of canals. So great will the sinking of New York be—according to Criswell—that New York's inhabitants will eventually be forced to abandon their city in favor of higher and drier land further inland.

The Irish clairvoyant Jim Gavin received practically the same psychic picture of the submergence of New York only a few years ago. He told how Staten Island would sink "like a raft being pulled under water," and foresaw lower Manhattan tipping into the bay, the waters reaching as far as 59th Street.

Geologists have known for many years that New York is, in fact, not built on very stable ground—although that ground is rocky. Commentator Hugh Allen [*Window in Providence*, 1943] made a disturbing observation, based on a study by William Hobbs described in "The Configuration of the Rock Floor of Greater New York," U.S. Geological Survey, Bulletin 270. Series B, Descriptive Geology, 73, 1905. According to Allen, because of the distribution of the various faults underlying New York, Manhattan Island would, in the event of an earthquake, "break up into three large chunks, destroying all the major New York landmarks, as well as seriously affecting its millions of inhabitants."

It is also disturbing to note that the fault-lines under New York City are part of a larger earth fracture which begins in the State of Maine and runs beneath regions of Boston and Philadelphia. In the third line of the first quatrain above, the French seer predicted that "two great rocks will war against each other" or "oppose one another for a long time." By the "two rocks" he may have meant the two lines of rock on either side of the New England fracture zone, which will oppose or push against one another in the upheaval.

Just how wide an area may be affected by the future New York quake may have been hinted at by the "sleeping seer" Edgar Cayce. In 1932, Cayce was asked what major earth movements could be expected in America in the future. While in trance, Cayce stated that alterations would occur in the west, central and eastern portions of the country, but that the greatest of these would be along the Atlantic coast. He specified later, in 1941, that the New York and the Connecticut areas are to be totally reshaped, with New York City to disappear completely. He also predicted that land farther to the south—portions of the states of North Caro-

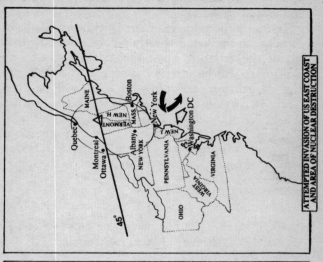

FAULT-LINES OF NEW YORK CITY

A. East River Fault
B. 125th Street Fault
C. Harlem River Fault
D. Dyckman Street Fault
E. Van Cortlandt Park Fault
F. Other major Faults

Central Park
Lincoln Center
Rockefeller Center
Empire State Building
Broadway
Wall Street
Brooklyn Bridge
Naval Shipyard
East River
Hudson River

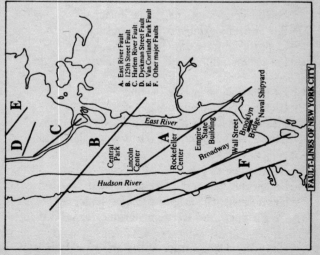

ATTEMPTED INVASION OF US EAST COAST AND AREA OF NUCLEAR DESTRUCTION

Quebec
Montreal
Ottawa
MAINE
Boston
MASS.
VERMONT
NEW H
New York
Albany
NEW YORK
PENNSYLVANIA
N J
Washington DC
OHIO
WEST VIRGINIA
VIRGINIA
45°

lina, South Carolina and Georgia—will also be inundated by water.

In much the same manner, British psychic John Pendragon predicted shortly before his death that all of the Atlantic coast region from Boston to Baltimore will be utterly destroyed. The center of the destruction, according to him, will be New York, but serious reverberations will be felt within a radius of 500 miles from the city. He also included Pittsburgh and Philadelphia in the destruction. Nothing will be left of these cities, Pendragon wrote, except the sunken sites where the cities once stood.

Q185–Q187. An Invasion of the United States Attempted Near New York

Le Roi voudra en cité neuve entrer,
Par ennemis expugner l'on viendra:
Captif libre faux dire et perpétrer,
Roi dehors être, loin d'ennemis tiendra. (IX,92)

La pille faite à la côte marine,
En cita nova et parents amenés,
Plusiers de Malte par le fait de Messine,
Étroit serrés seront mal geurdonnés. (IX,61)

Navale pugne suit sera superée,
Le feu auz naves à l'Occident ruine:
Rubriche neuve, la grande nef colorée,
Ire à vaincu, et victoire en bruine. (IX,100)

An army commander will want to march into the new city [New York City]

But because of his enemies he himself will be subdued.

The captive will act and speak falsely,

He will be kept outside the city, secure from help from his fellow countrymen.

The attack will be made on the sea coast,

At new city relatives brought forward.

When Malta is attacked from Messina [Sicily]

They will be closely confined, with no compensation.

Naval battle, when night is ending,

Fire from ships will cause ruin in the West [America]

Against them will come ships camouflaged in a new way,

The vanquished enemy angered; victory in a drizzle.

The Orientals will attempt to take advantage of the destruction and confusion that has beset the north-eastern coast of the United States because of the nuclear fire attack and earthquakes. They will regard this as the ideal time for a surprise invasion of America. Their landing will be preceded by a naval bombardment, followed by a landing attempt. The invasion will fail, however, when the US Navy counter-attacks with ships using newly developed anti-detection devices, and the commander of the invasion forces is captured. Similar to the protective measures taken during World War II, the USA will place those of Oriental extraction in "protective custody" during this time without any compensation whatsoever. Nostradamus sets the time for this invasion attempt during the same time period as when the Eastern forces in Sicily attack the island of Malta (Q70, Q115).

Q188. *The Eastern Invasion of Latin America*

En terre neuve bien avant Roi entré,
Pendant sujets lui viendront faire accueil:
Sa perfidie aura tel recontré,
Qu'aux citadins lieu de fête et recueil. (VII,74)

A military commander will invade deep into the New World [the Americas]
And some of his conquered subjects will welcome him.
But his revealed treachery will have such an effect
That the citizens will cancel a festive reception for his arrival.

While the Easterners will fail in their attempt to establish a beach-head near New York, they will be more successful in infiltrating the Latin American nations. One of the Latin American nations will plan to receive an Eastern commander as an honored guest, but a revelation of his treacherous acts will make the welcoming sympathizers realize how wrong they are in making an alliance with the power he represents, and they will cancel their planned meeting.

THE END OF THE WORLD

Q189. *The Murder of the President of Brazil*

Le fait luisant de neuf vieux élevé,
Seront si grands par Midi Aquilon:
De sa soeur propre grandes alles levé,
Fuyant meurtri au buisson d'Ambellon. (X,69)

A newly elected elder statesman will be placed
    in high position,
Against South Aquilon [South America] will
    come a great [military] force.
He [the statesman] will be raised by his sister;
    a leader of great crowds,
But fleeing, he will be murdered in the forests
    of Belem [Brazil].

The snubbing of the Eastern leader will in no way
change their plans for the conquest of Latin America, and the invasion plans will be carried out
according to schedule. A newly elected prominent
statesman of Brazil will attempt to escape the
Eastern troops but will be caught and murdered
near Belem in North-east Brazil.

Q190. *The Panama Canal Threatened*

De nuit par Nantes l'Iris apparaîtra,
Des arts marins susciteront la pluie:
Arabiq gouffre grande classe parfondra,
Un monstre en Saxe naître d'ours et truie.
(VI,44)

At night a rainbow will appear at Nantes
[north-east France],

167

By knowledge of the sea, they will stir up
   rain.
In the Gulf to Uraba [Darien, north Venezue-
   la], a great fleet will be sunk with swiftness,
When Saxony [East Germany] united with
   foreign powers.

The land invasion of Latin America will be backed
by a powerful fleet consisting of ships of the Eastern navy and the East German navy, but they
will be totally destroyed while approaching the
Panama Canal. Simultaneously, using their sophisticated knowledge of meterology, they [the East-
erners] are changing the weather patterns in France.

Q191. *The Northern Powers Retaliate with Germ Weapons*

Vent Aquilon fera partir le siège,
Pars murs jeter cendres, chaux et poussière:
Par pluie après, qui leur fera bien piege,
Dernier secours encontre leur frontière. (IX,99)

Aquilon [the nations of the north] will use
   the wind to end encirclement,
Beyond their defense lines they will launch
   forms of dust,
Rain will also disseminate it, which will once
   have been used against them,
This will be a desperate effort against their
   frontiers.

The United States and Russia will find themselves

totally surrounded by now, for the Easterners have managed to take Southern Asia, Africa, Europe and are expanding their hold in Latin America. Something desperate will have to be done, and they will choose a massive chemical/bacteriological attack against the East, in realiation for China's germ attack against them in the Arctic (Q29). No longer will the two "brothers of the north" feel bound to avoid the use of these horrible weapons. To them it may appear as the only way out of the stranglehold.

Q192–Q193. The Russians Take the Offensive

Le Roi rusé entendra ses embûches,
De trois quartiers ennemis assaillir:
Un nombre étrange larmes de coqueluches,
Viendra Lemprin du traducteur faillir. (IX,81)

La gent esclave par un heur martial
Viendra en haut degré tant elevée:
Changeront Prince, maîtra un provincial,
Passer la mer copie aux monts levée. (V,26).

The crafty commander will understand his enemy's entrapments,
His enemies will attack him from three directions.
A strange number of tears will come in the eyes of the coughing ones,
When the empire will fail the leader of the foreign language.

The Slavic people [Russians] will have good
  luck in the war,
They will gain a very powerful position.
Their leadership will change, from a Prince
  to one born in the country,
An army will leave the mountains, and pass
  over the seas.

The Soviet Union will be invaded by the Chinese
from three directions; from the south (Q30), from
the west and from conquered Europe, but the
Soviet commander will anticipate the enemy's strategy and will counter-attack with chemicals (Q191)
that will make the eyes of the enemy water uncon-
trollably. It will be a serious blow to the enemy
partly due to the fact that he does not receive all
the support he will need from the homeland.
Meanwhile, there will be a change in leadership
in the Russian government and there will be large
troop movements by sea.

Q194. *Eastern Penetration into the Pacific*

Sous l'opposite climat Babylonique,
Grande sera de sang effusion,
Que terre et mer, air, ciel sera inique:
Sectes, faim, regnes, pestes, confusion. (I,55)

In the place at antipodes to the Middle East
  [i.e. the South Pacific]
There will be a great outpouring of blood.
Evil forces will come by land and sea, by air
  in the sky,

And they will cause confusion, famine, disease among nations.

Realizing the strength of the Soviet Union and the United States, Eastern forces are setting up defenses in the Pacific to prepare for an all-out attack against Asia. Again we have the reference to disease, giving the distinct impression that their conquest of the Pacific islands will not only cause a great "outpouring of blood" but that it will be accomplished with the aid of bacteriological weapons.

Q195. The Battle for the Pacific

De mer copies en trois parts divisées,
À la seconde les vivres failliront,
Désespérés cherchant champs Helises,
Premiers en brèche entrés victoire auront. (IX,97)

The forces fighting at sea will be divided
among three nations,
The second of these will run out of supplies.
Surrounded by the third, and trying to reach
the Elysian Fields [America?],
But the first will find an opening in the
encirclement, and together they will win a
victory.

The fear of the Easterners was not ungrounded. The crucial battle to turn the tide of war will come at sea—and in the Pacific. During this battle, the American naval forces will find themselves surrounded and cut off from their supply bases in the United States. The Russian fleet will come to the rescue and will manage to break the Chinese stranglehold on the US Pacific fleet. The Chinese Navy will be defeated in the subsequent action, and together the two allies will break the Eastern control of the Pacific.

Q196. The First Major Eastern Defeat

Par deux fois haut, par deux fois mis à bas,
L'Orient aussi l'Occident faiblira:
Son adversaire après plusieurs combats,
Par mer chassé au besoin faillira. (VII,59)

Twice raised up, twice lowered,
The Orient will enfeeble the West.
Its adversary after several battles,
They will be defeated at sea and ultimately
    fail.

As in centuries past, when the Mongols and Muslims threatened Western civilizations and were defeated, so the same powers of the East will fail again after a second bid for world domination. But, this time, their defeat will first come by sea.

Q197. Nuclear Attack Against the Far East

L'oiseau royal sur la cité solaire,
Sept mois devant fera nocturne augure:
Mur d'Orient cherra tonnerre éclair,

THE END OF THE WORLD

Sept jours aux portes les ennemis à l'heure.
   (V,81)

The royal bird, [the Eagle, i.e. the United
   States] will be over the city of the sun
   [Rome],
It will appear as an omen that seven months
   later
The Oriental defense will fall amid lightning
   and noise,
For seven days the enemy will directly attack
   its gates.

By now the American/Russian offensive is well
under way, and the American air force will make
daring bombing runs into the heart of Eastern
Europe, going as far as Rome, the Eternal City.
Seven months later, the United States and the
Soviet Union will coordinate an attack against
China and her Far Eastern allies, and this barrage
will last a full week without ceasing.

Q198. *The Fall of China and Its Far Eastern Allies*

*Seront lors Seigneurs deux en nombre d'Aquilon,
victorieux sur les Orientaux, et sera en iceux fait
so grand bruikt et tumulte bellique, que tout
iceluis Orient tremblera de la frayeur de'iceux
frères, non frères Aquilonaires.*

*Sera par lors du principal chef Oriental la plupart
emu par les Septentroinaux et Occidentaux vaincu
et mis a mort profligez et le reste en fuite, et ses*

enfants de plusieurs femmes emprisonnés . . .
(Epistle to Henri II)

The leaders of Aquilon, two in number [the United States and Russia], will be victorious over the Orientals, and so great a noise and tumult of warfare will they produce that all the Orient will shake with terror because of these two brothers, who are not yet brothers.

The principal chief of the Orient will be vanquished by the Northerners [USA and Russia], and the Westerners [the Europeans], and the people they had stirred to war and had united with them will be put to death, overwhelmed and scattered, and their women and children will be made prisoners.

So the Allies have finally begun to show their superior firepower and are beginning to use it in the air, on the high seas, and on land. The Holocaust that ensued in the Pacific and in the Far East will bring the Far Eastern forces to their knees, and the war in the Far East will be finished before that in Europe and the Middle East. The defeat of the home base will, however, have definite psychological effects on the determination of the Easterners to hold on to Europe and the Middle East, for their supply line has now been cut.

Chapter 8

LIBERATION

Q199–Q202. A Second D-Day: Occupied Europe
Invaded

Comme un griffon viendra le Rois d'Europe,
Accompagné de ceux d'Aquilon:
De rouges et blancs conduira grande troupe,
Et iront contre le Roi de Babylon. (X,86)

Le camp Ascop d'Europe partira,
S'adjoignant proche de l'Isle submergée,
D'Arson classe phalange pliera,
Nombril du monde plus grande voix suborgée.
  (II,22)

L'Occident libre les Îles Britanniques,
Le reconnu passer le bas, puis haut,
Ne content triste Rebel corss. Escotiques
Puis reveller par plus et par nuit chaud. (VII,
  80,add.)

De l'Aquilon les efforts seront grands:
Sur l'Océan sera la porte ouverte,
Le regne en l'Île sera reintegrand:
Tremblera Londres par voile découverte. (II,68)

Like a winged griffon will come the commander of exiled European forces.
Accompanying him will be the commanders of Aquilon [USA and Russia].
They will lead a great army of red and white, And they will go against the commander of Babylon [the Middle East].

The incredible army of Europe will return from overseas,
And mass itself near the submerged Island [England],
The fleet will defeat a weak army
And at Rome a new leader will speak.

The Western powers will liberate the British Isles,
The recognized leader will return to power.
The discontented and sad rebel Scot,
Will attempt rebellion once more, in a warm season.

The efforts of the Aquilon [US-Russian] forces will be great:
They will gain an entrance on the Ocean coast.
The British will be restored to their island:
Those occupying London will tremble being discovered by ships.

A. Allied forces liberate the Isles of Scotland and London – Q201, Q202.
B. Defeat of Eastern naval forces – Q200.
C. Invasion of Scandinavia – Q203.
D. Russian offensive against occupied central Europe – Q203.
E. Allied invasion of south-west France – Q146-Q149, Q205.
F. Allied landing in northern France – Q204.

ISLE OF SCOTLAND

A

B

ISLE OF LONDON

A

NETHERLANDS

C

Calais

F

BELGIUM

St Quentin

D

FRANCE

La Rochelle

Bordeaux

E

ITALY

ALLIED INVASION OF OCCUPIED EUROPE

With the Far East out of the war except for mopping-up operations, the Western Allies are now concentrating their efforts on liberating Europe from Middle Eastern domination. The European forces that escaped to America, together with their Russian and American allies, will attack Europe from the air, striking against the Middle East forces. Western naval forces will rendezvous near the British Isles (Q64, Q65), and their coordinated air and sea strikes will defeat the Easterners occupying the Island of Scotland (Q161–Q165), and the Island City of London (Q166–Q169). The Scottish agitator will once more make an attempt to resist the British (Q161) but this will fail.

During this time, the Middle Eastern powers will have a new commander-in-chief who will establish his headquarters at Rome.

Q203–Q204. The Allied Strategy Against Eastern-held Europe

Norneigre et Dace, et l'Îsle Britannique,
Par les unis frères seront vexés:
Le chef Romain issu de sang Gallique
Et les copies aux forêts repoussées. (VI,7)

Lorsque celuis qu'à nul ne donne lieu,
Abandonner voudra lieu pris non pris:
Feu neuf par saignes, bitument à Charlieu,
Seront Quintin, Balex repris. (IX,29)

The enemy in Norway, in the Balkans and the British Isles,

Will be vexed by the united brothers [USA
and Russia]:
A Roman chief of French blood
And his forces will receive a setback in a
wooded area.

A leader who never retreated before anyone,
Will want to abandon a place he had just
occupied.
Fire from the ship igniting swamps, combus-
tibles at Charlieu,
Saint-Quentin and Clais recaptured.

The counter-offensive to liberate Britain will be
part of a three-pronged attack against the Easterners.
The second part of the attack will be directed
against Scandinavia and the Baltic states from the
north and from the Soviet Union. The third will
be from the Soviet Union against the Balkan
nations. Meanwhile, a European commander will
invade the European mainland near Calais, using
nuclear weapons, but he will meet heavy resistance in a wooded area, which will make him
wonder whether to make a strategic retreat.

Q205–Q207. The Allies Move Inland into France

Bordeaux, Rouan et la Rochelle joints,
Tiendront autour la grande mer Océan,
Anglois, Bretons, et les Flamans conjoints,
Les chasseront jusqu'auprès de Roane. (III,9)

Bien défendu le fait par excellence,

Gardes-toi Tours de ta proche ruine:
Londres et Nantes par Reims fera défense
Ne passe outre au temps de la bruine. (IV,46)

Le grand de foudre tombera d'heure diurne,
Mal, et prédit par porteur postulaire:
Suivant présage tombe de l'heure nocture,
Conflit Reims, Londres, Etrusque pestifère. (I,26)

The beach-heads at Bordeaux, La Rochelle
   [south-west France] and Rouen [north-west
   France] are secured,
And it will establish a hold on the Ocean
   coast.
By the Allied forces of the French, English
   and Dutch,
The enemy will be chased as far as Roanne
   [central France].

It is an established fact!
Those of Tours [west France], guard yourselves.
   Your ruin is near.
London [the British] will come from Nantes
   and fight against the defenders of Reims
   [north-east France],
But will be unable to proceed any further
   because of a drizzling rain.

The great commander of lightning weapons
   will die in the daytime,
Bad news will be brought to him by a negotiator.
A second prediction: another commander will
   die at night,

SWITZ

ITALY

FRANCE

SPAIN

Calais
St Quentin
Reims
Rouen
Paris
Sens
Nantes
Tours
Autun
La Rochelle
Roanne
Lyons
ALPS
Bordeaux
La Réole
Marmande
Guienne
Agen
Languedoc
Vernegues
Alleins
Durance
St Paul-de-Mausale
Foix
Narbonne
Salon
Nice
Marseilles
PYRENEES
LUBÉRON MTS
Barcelona

A
B
C
D
D
E
F
G
G
H
I
J

A. Allied forces liberate the north French coast – Q204.
B. Allied landing on the River Seine – Q205.
C. Offensive against Reims – Q206, Q207.
D. Loire-Rhône Valley penetration – Q205, Q206, Q208, Q212, Q214, Q215.
E. Allied offensive in south-west France – Q205, Q212, Q213.
F. Bombardment of Narbonne – Q216, Q217.
G. Eastern defeat at the Alps – Q209.
H. Seizure of the port of Barcelona – Q218.
I. Allied land and sea victory against Marseilles – Q219, Q220.
J. Port of Nice retaken – Q221.

LIBERATION OF FRANCE

When there is conflict at Reims [north-east
France], from London; there will be a plague
in Tuscany [Italy].

The area which the British will liberate in south-
west France (Q146–Q149) will be reinforced by
armies from the other Western powers. From a
second beach-head at La Rochelle up the coast,
the Allies will penetrate deep into central France
to Tours and then as far as the Roanne. A third
invasion force, landing near Calais (Q204) on the
north-western coast, will reach Rouen and proceed
to Reims in the north-eastern part of France. Bad
weather, however, will greatly slow down the offensive. One Eastern commander will die—probably of
a heart attack or suicide—when he receives bad
news; another commander will die during the night.

Q208–Q209. Central and Southern France Liberated

De sens, d'Autun viendront jusqu'au Rosne,
Pour passer outree vers les monts Pyrénées:
La gent sortir de la Marche l'Anconne:
Par terre et mer suivra a grandes trainées. (II,74)

Dans le Danube et de Rhin viendra boire
Le grand Chemeau, ne s'en repentira:
Trembler du Rosne, et plus fort ceux de Loire,
Et prés des Alpes Coq de luinera. (V,68)

From Sens [north central France], and Autun
[east France], they will come as far as the
Rhône,

Others to pass beyond °toward the Pyrenees
  mountains.
Forces to leave Ancona [east Italy] for defense,
By land and sea they will be followed by great
  noise.

In the rivers Danube and Rhine will come to
  drink
The great Camel [the Arabs], who will not be
  sorry.
They will make those of the rivers Rhône and
  Loire tremble,
But near the Alps the French will ruin them.

Allied forces in northern France will push southward toward the river Rhône, and a French army
will defeat the Easterners near the Alps. This will
occur when the Easterners have occupied Austria,
Germany (Q172–Q174), and south-east France
(Q103–Q104). A second Allied force in south-
west France (Q205) will attack Eastern forces
entrenched in the Pyrenees as the first step to an
invasion of Spain. Meanwhile, Eastern armies from
Italy will be hastily sent to form a defensive line
against the steadily advancing Allied thrust into
France.

Q210–Q211. The Middle Eastern Strategy— Continued Resistance

En lieu bien proche non éloigné de Venise,
Les deux plus grands de l'Asie et d'Affrique,
Du Rhin, et Hister qu'on dira sont venus,

Cris, pleurs à Malte et côté Ligustique. (IV,68)

Les deux contents seront unis ensemble,
Quand le plupart à Mars seront conjoint:
Le grand d'Affrique en effrayeur tremble,
Duumvirat par la classe déjoint. (V,23)

In a location not far from Venice,
The leaders of conquered Asia and Africa
    will meet
After taking the Rhine and the lower Danube,
Cries and tears at Malta and Genoa.

Two powers contented because of conquest
    will be united together,
And together will be joined in Mars [war].
But then the great leaders of Africa will shake
    in terror,
When the union will be broken by the oppos-
    ing fleet.

Not long after the Easterners capture southern
Europe and defeat the nations of Germany and
Austria (Q172–Q174), the Far Eastern and Middle Eastern conquerors will hold a strategy confer-
ence near Venice. But after the Eastern defeat in
the Pacific (Q196), and the downfall of China
(Q197–Q198), the union between the two conquerors will be at an end. The forces of the Middle
Eastern powers and those of the Far Eastern powers still in Europe will stand alone in their attempt
to keep Europe from falling back into the hands of
the Western armies.

THE END OF THE WORLD
Q212–Q215. The Conflict in Southern France

Passer Guienne, Languedoc et le Rosne,
D'Agen tenant de Marmande et la Roole:
D'ouvrier par foi parroy, Phocen tiendra son
  trône,
Conflit auprès sainct Pol de Mauseole. (IX,85)

Plaintes et pleurs, cris et grands hurlemants,
Près de Narbon à Bayonne et en Foix
O quels horribles calamités changements,
Avant que Mars révolu quelques fois. (IX,63)

Quand seront proches le defaut des lunaires,
De l'un a l'autre ne distant grandement,
Froid, siccite, danger vers les frontières,
Même où l'oracle a pris commencement. (III,4)

Aux champs herbeux d'Alein et du Varneigne
De mont Lebron proche de la Durance,
Champs de deux parts conflit sera si aigre,
Mesopatamie défaillira en la France. (III,99)

They will march from Guienne to Languedoc
  [south-west France] toward the Rhône,
And will hold Agen, Marmande, and La Réole
  [south-west France]:
In the hope of finding a way to Marseilles,
  the major base of the enemy.
There will be conflict [war] near Saint-Paul-
  de-Mausole [south-east France].

Anger, tears, cries and howls,

Near Narbonne, Bayonne [on the Mediterra-
nean coast] and Foix.
Oh what horrible calamities and changes.
Mars [war] will affect them several times.

When fighting will come close to here, the
lunar ones [Arabs] will fail.
From one to another at no great distance,
Suffering from cold, dryness, and the danger
of the enemy pushing at their frontiers,
Where this prophecy had its beginnings [Salon-
en-Provence, south-east France].

In the grassy fields of Alleins and Vernegues,
In the Luberon range and near the river
Durance [all in south-east France],
The conflict will be sharp for both sides,
But in the end the Mesopotamians [the Mid-
dle Easterners] will be defeated in France.

From the British positions in south-west France,
the Allies will penetrate up the river Garonne
toward the Mediterranean coast. Western forces in
north-east France will also drive down the river
Rhône toward the Mediterranean. The aim of
both invasion forces will be to reach Marseilles,
the Easterners' stronghold and supply port and
staging area in southern France. Nostradamus foresaw that important battles will be fought very near
his hometown of Salon-en-Provence, in south-east
France.

Classe Gauloise par appui de grande garde
Du grand Neptune, et ses tridents soldats,
Rougée Provence pour soutenir grande bande:
Plus Mars Narbon, par javelots et dards. (II,59)

Le grand Neptune de profond de la mer,
De gent Punique et sang Gaulois mêlé.
Les Îles à sang, pour le tardif ramer:
Plus lui nuira que l'occulte mal célé. (II,78)

A French fleet will be supported by an impressive land force,
Also from beneath the sea, Neptune and his sea forces will come,
Provence [south-east France] will be reddened, to be occupied by a great host,
Destruction at Narbonne because of flying projectile weapons.

The forces of great Neptune will come from beneath the sea
When North African and French blood are mixed in battle.
The Isles [Corsica and Sardinia] will bleed; not reached in time. ·
This setback will hurt him, because of a secret not well kept.

The Allied drive on southern France by land will be coordinated with a submarine attack on the Mediterranean coast. The French city of Narbonne (Q213) in particular will suffer greatly from an attack with guided missiles. The same submarine force will also attempt an invasion of Corsica and Sardinia, but the attack will fail because of a security lead.

Q218–Q220. *The Fall of Eastern-held Marseilles*

Par le grand Prince limitrophe du Mans,
Preux et vaillant chef du grand excercite:
Par mer et terre de Gallots et Normans,
Calpre passer Bardelonne pillé l'île. (VII,10)

De Barcelonne par mer si grande armée,
Toute Marseille de frayeur tremblera:
Îles saisies de mer aide fermée,
Ton traditeur en terre nagera. (III,88)

L'ordre fatal sempiternel par chaîne
Viendra tourner par ordre consequent,
Du port Phocen sera rompue la chaîne:
La cité prise, l'ennemis quand et quand. (III,79)

A great leader from near Le Mans [south France],
A doughty and valiant chief of a great army,
Will come by land and sea with British and northern French forces,
He will pass Gibraltar, take Barcelona [east Spain] and attack the Isles [Corsica and Sardinia].

From Barcelona will come a very great army by sea,

THE END OF THE WORLD

All of Marseilles will tremble with fear.
When the Isles [Corsica and Sardinia] are
seized and help is shut off by sea,
A traitor will swim on land [drown in his
own blood].

The final order for destruction of the defenses,
Will be passed down, and its consequences
The defenses of Marseilles will be broken.
The city taken, and the enemy captured at
the same time.

A French army general will return to fight accompanied by the British forces as well as the northern French army. He will enter near Gibraltar; seize the Spanish port of Barcelona, and from there prepare for an attack on the Eastern base at Marseilles (Q212). In preparation for this attack, the Allied taskforce will first move on Corsica and Sardinia (Q127) and succeed in taking the islands. Through this action the Allies will effectively cut off the supply lines to Marseilles. The spy who caused the first attempt to fail (Q217) will be located and executed. The assault on Marseilles will be successful, and the Eastern occupation force will surrender to the French/British army.

Q221. The Port of Nice Retaken

Grand Roi viendra prendre port près de Nisse,
Le grand empire de la mort si en fera:
Aux Antipolles posera sa génisse,
Par mer la Pille tout évanouira. (X,87)

A great military commander will capture the port
   of Nice [south French coast],
There will be a severe blow to the Arab empire.
In Antibes the commander will place a monument
   of victory.
Eventually the plunder by sea will vanish.

One of the Allied armies will reach the Riviera
and take control of the city of Nice. It will be a
severe blow to the Arabs for, by liberating this
port, the Allies will end Eastern control of the
Western Mediterranean.

Q222–Q224. The Eastern Counter-offensive Against Southern France

La tour de Boucq craindra fuste Barbare,
Un temps, longtemps après barque Hesperique:
Bétail, gens, meubles, tous deux feront grand tare,
Taurus et Libra, quelle mortelle pique! (I,28).

La tour marine trois fois prise et reprise
Par Espagnols, Barbares, Ligurins:
Marseille et Aix, Arles par ceux de Pise,
Vast feu, fer, pille Avignon des Thurins. (I,71)

Au chef Anglois à Nîmes trop séjour,
Devers l'Espagne au secours Aenobarbe:
Plusiers mourrant par Mars ouvert ce jour,
Quand en Artois faillir étoile en barbe. (V,59)

The tower of Bouc [south French coast] will
   fear the Arab fleet

But much later will come the Hesperian
    [American] ships.
Cattle, people and goods will be destroyed;
Muslims and Christians—what a deadly quarrel!

The tower on the coast will three times be
    taken and retaken
By Arabs from Spain and Italy.
They will counter-attack against Marseilles,
    and Aix-en-Provence, [south-east France],
Devastation by fire, metal weapons, Avignon
    pillage from Turin [north-west Italy].

An English chief will tarry too long at Nîmes
    [north France],
Another chief named Redbeard will come to
    the rescue by marching toward Spain,
Many will die from a war started that day,
When a streaming star will fall on Artois
    [north France].

The Arabs will take the offensive by attacking
from Spain and Italy, and recapturing parts of
southern and south-eastern France. A decisive naval
battle will be fought near a tower at Bouc, on the
coast. A British commander will find himself
besieged in the city of Nîmes, but another western
commander named Redbeard will end the encirclement by destroying the Arab supply lines from
Spain. At the same time the Arabs will launch a
missile attack against Allied forces stationed near
Artois [north France].

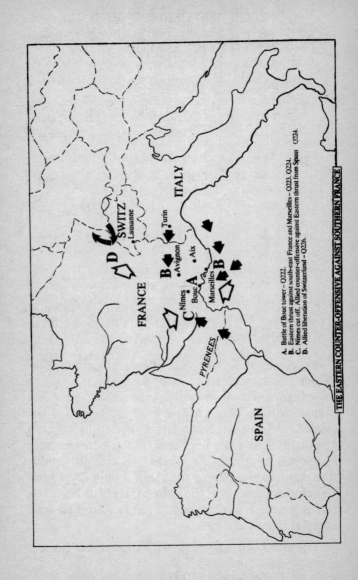

THE EASTERN COUNTER-OFFENSIVE AGAINST SOUTHERN FRANCE

A. Battle of Bouc tower – 0222.
B. Eastern thrust against south-east France and Marseilles – 0223, 0224.
C. Nimes cut off, Allied counter-offensive against Eastern thrust from Spain   0224.
D. Allied liberation of Switzerland – 0226.

SWITZ
Lausanne
ITALY
Turin
FRANCE
Avignon
Aix
Nimes
Bouc
Marseilles
B
A
C
D
B
PYRENEES
SPAIN

Q225. The Counter-offensive Fails—The Easterners Driven Back

L'ennemi docte se trouvera confus,
Grand camp malade, et défait par embûches,
Monts Pyrénées et Poenus lui seront faits refus,
Proche du fleuve découvrant antiques cruches.
  (VI,99)

The knowledgeable enemy will be lost and
  confused,
His great army will be sick, and defeated by
  constant ambushes.
He will lose control of the Pyrenees and
  Apennine mountains,
Finding only funerary urns near a river.

The Arabs are on the run. Their offensive in France will fail miserably, and their army will end diseased and disoriented. The Allies will take advantage of this by pushing the Arab forces out of France across the Pyrenees, and also into Italy.

Q226. Germ and Nuclear Weapons Used Against Switzerland

Puanteur grande sortira de Lausanne,
Qu'on ne saura l'origine du fait,
L'on mettra hors toute la gent lointaine,
Feu vu au ciel, peuple étranger défait. (VII,10)

A foul smell will come out of Lausanne [west
  Switzerland],

193

None will know which side will have launched
   it;
They will the armies from afar to withdraw,
Fire will be seen in the sky; the foreign people will be defeated.

Using eastern France as a staging area, the Westerners will attempt to liberate Switzerland, but
with terrible consequences for the city of Lausanne.
It will be the target of bacteriological weapons,
and the Arabs will retreat, but not before they
have unleashed their atomic weapons in the skies
over the city.

Q227. Spain Reconquered

Dans les Espaignes viendra Roi très-puissant,
Par mer et terre subjuguant le Midi:
Ce mal fera rebaissant le croissant,
Baisser les ailes à ceux du Vendredi. (X,95)

A great and powerful leader will attack the
   Spanish lands,
By land, and sea, he will conquer toward the
   south.
This evil will lower again the power of the
   crescent [the Arabs],
And will clip the wings of flight of those who
   worship on Friday [Muslims].

Crossing the Pyrenees from France, a Western general will recapture Spain and destroy several strategic Arab air bases, thereby grounding the airforce

and keeping the Middle Eastern army from fleeing by air.

Q228–Q229. Naval Battles Off the West Coast of Italy

Qu'en dans poisson, fer et lettre enfermée,
Hors sortira qui puis fera la guerre,
Aura par mer sa classe bien ramée,
Apparaissant près de Latine terre. (II,5)

De vaine emprise l'honneur indue plainte,
Galiotes errants par Latins, froids, faim, vagues
Non loin du Tymbre de sang la terre teinte,
Et sur humains seront diverses plagues. (V,63)

When iron [Mars] and a letter [Mercury] are
    enclosed in a fish [Pisces]
One will leave to make war.
His fleet will be well propelled by sea,
Appearing near Latin land [Italy].

An unsuccessful enterprise will bring honor
    to some, undue complaints for others,
Ships will be engaged in Latin seas [off Italy],
    to suffer cold, hunger and great waves,
Not far from the Tiber [Rome] the land will
    be stained with blood,
And diverse diseases will inflict [damage] on
    everyone.

Allied and Eastern fleets will engage in a naval battle not far off the Italian coast, and both will

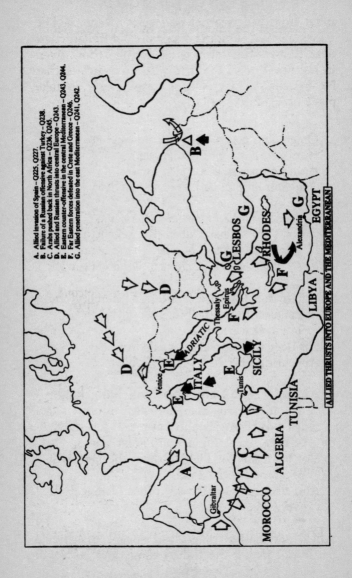

A. Allied invasion of Spain – Q225, Q227.
B. Failure of a Russian offensive against Turkey – Q238.
C. Arabs pushed back in North Africa – Q234, Q245.
D. Allied and Russian thrusts into central Europe – Q243.
E. Eastern counter-offensive in the central Mediterranean – Q243, Q244.
F. Far Eastern forces defeated in Crete and Greece – Q246.
G. Allied penetration into the east Mediterranean – Q241, Q242.

ALLIED THRUSTS INTO EUROPE AND THE MEDITERRANEAN

MOROCCO
ALGERIA
TUNISIA
LIBYA
EGYPT

Gibraltar
Tunis
SICILY
ITALY
Venice
ADRIATIC
Thessaly
Epirus
LESBOS
RHODES
Alexandria

suffer from bad weather and germ weapons. The Allies will also conduct a raid on the Italian coast near Rome. The astrological configuration given in the first line of the first quatrain indicates that Nostradamus expected this naval battle to take place on 3 March 1996.

Q230–Q233. *The Allied Offensive Against Italy*

Naples, Palerme, Sicile, Syracuses,
Nouveaux tyrans, fulgares feux célestes:
Force de Londres, Gand, Bruxelles et Suses,
Grand hécatombe, triomphe faire festes. (II,16)

Pendant qu'l'Aigle et le Coq à Savone,
Seront unis, Mer, Levant et Ongrie:
L'armée a Naples, Palerme, Marque d'Ancone,
Rome, Venise par Barbe horrible cri. (VII,9)

Champ Perusin ô l'énorme défaite,
Et le conflit tout auprès de Ravenne:
Passage sacre lorsque'on fera la fête,
Vainqueur vaincu cheval manger l'aveine. (VII,72)

Le grand mené captif d'étrange terre,
D'or enchaîne au Roi Chyren offert:
Qui dans Ausone, Milan perdra la guerre,
Et tout son ost mis à feu et à fer. (IV,34)

Naples [Italy], Palermo, Syracuse and all of
    Sicily,
Dominated by Arab tyrants who will conquer
    them with fires and lightning from the sky,

197

Then will come forces from London [the British], Ghent and Brussels [Belgium] by way of Susa [north Italy],

There will be great slaughter; then triumph will lead to festivities.

While the Eagle [United States] and the Cock [French] at Savona [north-west Italy]

Will be united; they will launch an attack by sea against the Middle East and against Hungary,

The army will reach Naples [west Italian Coast], and Ancona [east coast] and Palermo [Sicily].

Because of the Arabs, there will be a great outcry from Rome and Venice.

Oh what an enormous defeat on the fields of Perugia [central Italy].

And another conflict near Ravenna [north-east Italy].

Passage given to the religious to celebrate a feast,

Once conqueror, now vanquished, they will eat horseflesh.

A great leader of the foreign nation will now be a prisoner

Chained in gold and brought to General Henry.

He who in Ausonia [south Italy] and at Milan will lose the battle,

And all his forces burned with fiery weapons.

A. Invasion of Corsica and Sardinia – Q218, Q219.
B. Allied raid on coast near Rome – Q229.
C. Sea and land strike against north-west Italy – Q230, Q231, Q233.
D. Eastern defeat at Milan – Q233.
E. Penetration into central Italy – Q231, Q232.
F. Eastern defeat in southern Italy – Q231, Q233.
G. Liberation of Rome – Q234, Q235.
H. Invasion of Sicily – Q230, Q231.
I. Allied attempt to invade Yugoslavia – Q237, Q238.

RECONQUEST OF ITALY

Western forces will defeat Arab armies in northern Italy by land and unite with American naval forces at Savona, in north-west Italy. From there, they will proceed down the coast to Naples, and also across the Italian boot to Ancona by way of Perugia and Ravenna. Venice and Rome will be bombed. An Eastern leader who will be defeated at Milan and lose command over southern Italy will be brought before an Allied leader named Henry. At the same time, the Russian offensive against the Balkan nations (Q203) will move on into Hungary.

Q234–Q235. The Church Returned to Liberated Rome

De sang Troyen naîtra coeur Germanique,
Qui deviendra en si haute puissance:
Hors chassera gent étrange Arabique,
Tournant l'Eglise en pristine prééminence. (V,74)

Le grand Celtique entrera dedans Rome,
Menant amas d'exilés et bannis:
Le grand Pasteur mettra à mort tout homme,
Qui pour le coq étaient aux Alpes unis. (VI,28)

Of French blood will be born one of German
   background,
He will rise to very great military power.
He will be instrumental in driving out the
   foreign and Arab peoples,
And he will return the Church to Rome, to
   its former power.

The great Frenchman will enter Rome,

Leading a throng of exiles and banished citizens.

The great Pontiff will order the death of all those who were

United with the enemy at the Alps against the French.

A French general of German background will overwhelm the Arab headquarters at Rome (Q200), and will help re-establish the Church in its former seat of power. The Pope will order the execution of those Italian sympathizers who fought with the Arabs against the French at the Battle of the Alps (Q209); and he can do this in his function of head of the Italian government.

As far back as the early Christian era, there have been numerous predictions about a time when a French king or great military leader will defeat the Muslims in a major world war and restore a Pope to his rightful throne.

An early psychic, Sain Cesar (AD 470–542) predicted that there would someday be a war in which Paris, Marseilles, Bordeaux and other prominent French cities would be destroyed, but that soon afterward would come a "Great King" and a "great Pontiff" from France who would change the world.

Prophet Aimon of Hyppolitus foresaw ". . . the great French monarch, who shall subjugate all the East, shall come about the end of the world."

Another ancient psychic of England, Merlin the Magician, is attributed with the prediction that "a king of the French, with his people," will someday "restore the rightful Pope" . . . and identified the future French leader as the "last king of France" before the end of the world. Can this possibly mean that he expects France to return a monarch to the throne around the time of World War III?

Abbott Werdin made a forecast that contains a specific time element, as far back as the thirteenth century. He predicted that "The nations will be at war for four years, and a great part of the world will be destroyed. All the sects will vanish. The capital of the world [Rome] will fall. The Pope will cross the sea. The Great Monarch will then come to restore peace, and the Pope will share in the victory of the Great Monarch."

Commented Davis Poreaus, who died in 1657, "The Great Monarch will be of French descent, large forehead, large dark eyes, light brown wavy hair, and an eagle nose. He will crush the enemies of the Pope and will conquer the East."

With the conquest of Europe almost completed, the Western forces will now turn against the homelands of the enemy, the Middle Eastern countries, and carry the way to the ultimate staging areas.

Chapter 9

THE FINAL CONFLICT—WAR IN THE MIDDLE EAST

Q236. *Arab Defeat in North Africa*

De Barcelone, de Gennes et Venise,
De la Secille peste Monet unis:
Contre Barbare classe prendront la vise,
Barbare poussé bien loin jusque'à Thunis.
(IX,42)

Allies at the ports of Barcelona [Spain], Genoa
    and Venice [Italy],
Disease-stricken Monaco and Sicily,
Together they will coordinate action against
    the Arab fleet,
The Arabs will be driven back into Tunisia.

The Allies will push the Arab forces completely
out of western Europe and the western Mediterranean, and in North Africa, they will be repulsed
as far east as Tunisia.

Q237–Q238. Allied Disaster in the Adriatic

Au port de Pyola et de sainct Nicolas,
Périr Normande au gouffre phanatique:
Cap. de Bisance rues crier hélas,
Secours de Gaddes et du grand Philippique.
  (IX,30)

Par feu et armes non loin de la marnegro,
Viendra de Perse occuper Tribesonde:
Trembler Pharos, Methelin, Sol alegro,
De sang Arabe d'Adrie couvert onde. (V,27)

At the port of Pola and San Nicole [Yugo-
  slavian coast],
And in the coast of Quarnero [the Adriatic]
  the French will die.
The captives in Turkey will cry in despair,
But help will come from Cadiz [Spain] from a
  leader named Philip.

Through fiery arms they will invade the Black
  Sea area,
They will come from Iran to occupy Trebson
  [east Turkey]
But others will take Pharos [Alexandria, Egypt]
  and Mytilene [Island of Lesbos, off Turkey]
  the sun shining brightly,
The Adriatic Sea covered with Arab blood.

The counter-offensive against the Arabs is beginning to gain momentum and, with northern Italy
as base, the French will try to cross the Adriatic
and land on the north-west coast of Yugoslavia.

But the French forces will be annihilated, or taken captive to Turkey. The Arabs will also suffer serious losses, and not only in the Adriatic area. The Western Allies will begin forcing their way into the eastern Mediterranean by seizing the islands off Turkey and striking against Egypt. The Arabs, however, will push a part of the attacking force back into the Soviet Union.

Q239–Q240. A Daring Raid to Free Prisoners of War

La barbe crêpe et noire par engin,
Subjuguera la gent cruelle et fière:
Le grand Chyren ôtera du longin
Tous les captifs par Seline bannière. (II, 79).

Des régions sujettes à la Balance,
Feront troubler les monts par grande guerre,
Captifs tout sexe dû et tout Bisance,
Qu'on criera à l'aube terre à terre. (V, 70)

The Arab with the black and frizzled hair, by his skill
Will with boasting and cruelty imprison many peoples.
But the great Henry will travel far to free and remove them,
All those captured by the banner of the Moon [the Arabs].

From the regions subject to the Balance [Italy]
Forces in the mountains will cause great war.

Captives of both sexes in Turkey will suddenly be overjoyed.

And at dawn the news of the fear will spread from nation to nation.

While the Allies will occupy the Alps and the Apennine mountains of Italy, an Allied commander named Henry (Q233) will secretly invade Turkey to free the Allied prisoners of war held there (Q237). The raid will liberate both male and female prisoners, and will be an unqualified success. It will be broadcast all around the world.

Q241–Q242. *Penetration into the Eastern Mediterranean*

À son haut prix plus la larme sabee,
D'humaine chair par mort en cendre mettre,
A l'île Pharos par Croissars perturbée,
Alors qu'a Rhodes paraîtra du espectre. (V,16)

Le vieux monarque déchassé de son regne
Aux Orients son secours ira querre:
Pour peur des croix pliera son enseigne:
En Mytilene ira par port et terre. (III,47)

An attack on southern Arabia will be launched,
Weapons of death turning human flesh to ashes.
The Island of Pharos [north Egypt] attacked by the Crusaders,
The Isle of Rhodes [in the Aegean] will be restored.

The older leader will be chased out of his
   realm,
He will flee to the East for help.
For fear of the crosses [Christian western forc-
   es], he will fold his banner [surrender],
And will go to Mytilene [Lesbos], to the port
   and then by land.

Simultaneously with the Western thrust into the
east Mediterranean and against Egypt (Q238), the
Allies will use a "disintegration weapon" against
southern Arabia which will turn human flesh to
ashes. Also a European leader who defected to the
East will surrender himself to the Allied invasion
force that will be landing at Lesbos.

Q243–Q244. *The Eastern Counter-offensive;
Recapture of Sicily*

*Voile Symacle port Massiliolique,
Dans Venise port marcher aux Pannons:
Partir du gouffre et sinus Illirique,
Vast à Socille, Ligurs coupe de canons.* (IX,28)

*Le neuf empire en desolation,
Sera changé de pôle aquilonaire:
De la Socille viendra l'émotion,
Troubler, l'emprise à Philip tributaire.* (VII,81)

The Allied transport fleet will leave the port
   of Marseilles,
In the port of Venice they will unload those
   who will march against the Balkans.

But they will be unable to leave the Adriatic,
The enemy will destroy Sicily and bombard
   the north-west coast of Italy.

The newly conquered empire, now in desola-
   tion,
Because of help from those of Aquilon [USA
   and Russia]
At Sicily they will make a comeback,
Troubling the advance of a commander named
   Philip.

The advancing Western forces will make a drive
into central Europe from the direction of north-
east Italy. Their object will be to join Russian
troops fighting in the same area (Q203, Q231),
and cut the remaining Eastern forces in Europe in
half. Meanwhile, the Arabs will attempt to halt
the Western infiltrations into the eastern Mediterranean by blocking the Adriatic, destroying Western positions on Sicily, and raiding supply lines
originating from ports on the north-west Italian
coast.

The commander named Philip, who lost to the
Easterners in north-west France (Q124), and came
to the aid of the victims of the Adriatic disaster
(Q237), will be involved in the battles for Italy
and Sicily.

*Q245. The Offensive Fails—the Liberation of
Central Europe*

Par grande fureur le Roi Romain Belgique,

THE END OF THE WORLD

Vexer voudra par phalange barbare:
Fureur grinçant, chassera gent Lybique,
Depuis Pannons jusques Hercules la hare. (V,13)

With great fury, a Roman and a Belgian leader,
Will vex the Arabs and their forces.
With furious hatred he will chase the African
  people,
From Gibraltar and from the Balkans.

Eventually, the Arab offensive in the central Mediterranean will fail and, led by a Roman and a Belgian general, the Arabs will taste defeat, and the Balkans and central Europe will be liberated.

Q246. *Far Eastern Forces Defeated in Crete and Greece*

Le chef qu'aura conduit peuple infini,
Loin de son ciel, du moeurs et langue étrange:
Cinq mil en Crete et Thessalie fini,
Le chef fuyant suavé en marine grange. (I,98)

A chief who will have led a countless number
  of people,
Of strange languages and tongues, by air from
  other skies,
Five thousand of them will die in Crete and
  Thessaly [east Greece],
The chief will escape in an enclosure, travel-
  ling by sea.

Despite the defeat of China, several Far Eastern

armies will still be fighting with the Arabs under their own general, but they will not be able to halt the Western offensive. Five thousand of them will die fighting in Crete and in Eastern Greece— and, seeing the futility of it all, their commanding officer will escape surrender by submarine.

Q247. A Rebellion Among the French Commanders

Sept ans sera Philip, fortune prospère,
Rebaissera des Arabes l'effort:
Puis son midi perplexe rebours affaire,
Jeune ogmion abîmera son fort. (IX,89)

For seven years a commander named Philip will be very fortunate,
He will be one of those who will check the advances of the Arabs.
But at high-point of his career, something very perplexing will happen,
For a French general named Ogmios will revolt, destroy his base and take over his command.

It appears that General Philip will find himself in serious trouble when, at the height of his career, a French general named Ogmios will lead a rebellion of Philip's troops and take over Philip's command. This change in command does not seem to have any consequences that will affect the outcome of the war.

THE END OF THE WORLD
Q248–Q250. The Allied Assault on Turkey

Les plus grand voile hors du port de Zara,
Près de Bisance fera son enterprise:
D'ennemi perte et l'ami ne sera,
Le tiers à deux fera grand pille et prise. (VIII,83)

Parmi les champs des Rodanes entrées,
Où les croisés seront presque unis,
Les deux brassières en pisces recontrées,
Et un grand nombre par déluge punis. (VIII,91)

L'ogmion grande Bisance approchera,
Chassée sera la Berbarique Ligue,
Des deux lois l'une l'estinique lâchera,
Barbare et France en perpétuelle brigue. (V,80)

The great leader of the fleet will leave the
port of Zara [Yugoslavia],
Near Turkey will he carry out his orders.
Loss of life through battle on both sides will
not take place,
Instead a storm will inflict damage on both
sides.

Entering the fields of battle near Rhodes [in
the Aegean],
The crusading Allies will almost be united.
Mars and Venus in Pisces,
A great number will die in a flood of
water.

The French general Ogmios will attack Turkey,
The Arab defenders will be driven out.

Of the two religions, the heathen one [Mo-
hammedanism] will give way,
Arabs and French will be in a [seemingly]
never-ending battle.

Ogmios's take-over from General Philip seems to
have the approval of the High Command for,
soon after his military coup d'état, he will make a
bold attack on Turkey, where he will drive the
Arab defenders back beyond the borders. While he
is fighting in Turkey, a Western fleet will leave the
Adriatic in order to attack the Arab fleet off
Turkey. But the expected battle between the two
fleets will not take place, instead they will suffer
the devastating effects of a terrible storm in which
ships on both sides will be lost.

Q251–Q252. Landing Made in Southern Turkey

La grand cité de Tharse par Gaulois
Sera détruite, captifs tous à Turban,
Secours par mer du grand Portugalois,
Premier d'été le jour du sacre Urban. (VI,85)

Après séjourné vagueront en Epire,
La grand secours viendra vers Antioche,
La noir poil crêpe tendra fort à l'Empire:
Barbe d'airain le rôtira en broche. (I,74).

The great city of Tarsus [south Turkey] will
be destroyed
By the French, all the Arabs will be captured.

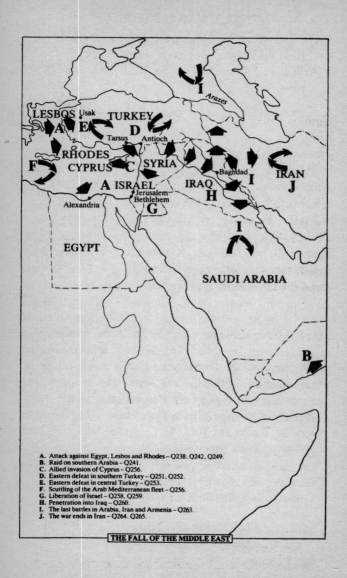

LESBOS Usak TURKEY
A E D
Tarsus Antioch
RHODES
CYPRUS C SYRIA
F Baghdad
A ISRAEL IRAQ IRAN
Jerusalem- H J
Bethlehem
Alexandria G

EGYPT

SAUDI ARABIA B

Araxes

A. Attack against Egypt, Lesbos and Rhodes – Q238. Q242, Q249.
B. Raid on southern Arabia – Q241.
C. Allied invasion of Cyprus – Q256.
D. Eastern defeat in southern Turkey – Q251, Q252.
E. Eastern defeat in central Turkey – Q253.
F. Scuttling of the Arab Mediterranean fleet – Q256.
G. Liberation of Israel – Q258, Q259.
H. Penetration into Iraq – Q260.
I. The last battles in Arabia, Iran and Armenia – Q263.
J. The war ends in Iran – Q264. Q265.

THE FALL OF THE MIDDLE EAST

Aid will come by sea from the great leader of
  Portugal,
From Urban's day of consecration to the first
  day of summer.

After being slowed down, they will reach
  Epirus [Greece].
A great effort will be made against Antioch
  [south Turkey]
The enemy leader with the black frizzled hair
  will strive with great energy to save his
  empire,
But the commander named Redbeard will burn
  him with fire.

Between 25 May and 21 June, the French will
make an assault on Turkey's southern coast at
Tarsus and Antioch. A number of Arab prisoners
will be taken. At the same time Allied armies will
meet heavy resistance in Greece. The Arab commander with the black frizzled hair who fought in
Italy against the French and who took many of
them captive (Q60, Q239), will hold his positions
in the hope of buying time to reorganize the Arab
defense line. His obstinacy will force the Western
General Redbeard (Q224) to annihilate him and
his armies with fire [nuclear?].

Q253. Resistance in Northern Turkey

Au grand de Cheramon agora,
Seront croisés par rang rous attachés,
Le pertinax Oppo, et Mandragora,

214

THE END OF THE WORLD

Raugon d'Octobre le tiers seront lâchés. (IX,62)

Against the great leader of Usak [central
    Turkey]
Will come the crusaders with new reinforce-
    ments.
The enemy leaders Oppi and Mandragora will
    hold for a long time,
But on the third of October, the River Bender-
    ik will be crossed.

Although Redbeard burned the Black Frizzled One
and General Ogmios has driven the main Arab
armies to beyond the borders, the army in Anatolia
is still holding on, and Western forces coming
from the southern part of Turkey penetrate deep
into the center of the Turkish heartland, and will
meet stubborn resistance from Arab [?] Generals
Oppi and Mandragora. They will not be defeated
until the third of October.

Q254. An Allied Invasion Attempt Fails

Proche à descendre l'armée Crucigere,
Sera guettée par les Ismaëlites,
De tous côtés battus par nef Raviere,
Prompt assaillis de dix galères élites. (IX,43)

Just as the crusading army is making a landing,
It will be ambushed by Arab forces.
It will be struck from every direction; the
    flagship Impetuosity
Attacked by ten fast ships!

One of the Western amphibious landing attempts will fail because of a murderous fire directed at it from every direction by the defending Arab forces. The flagship of the fleet will be attacked by ten enemy ships simultaneously.

Q255. *Arab Saboteurs Destroy an Allied Base*

Sur le combat des grand chevaux légers,
On criera le grand croissant confond:
De nuit tuer monts, habits de bergers,
Abîmes rouges dans le fossé profond. (VII, 7)

There will be a battle involving large but
    light horses,
The outcome will bring defeat to the great
    crescent [the Arabs],
But by night they will return dressed as shep-
    herds in the mountains to kill,
Pools of blood in the valley.

Light armored vehicles of the Western side will be victorious in a major battle against the Arabs. They do not take their losses lightly, and will send Arab terrorists to penetrate Western lines and create havoc and destruction at a military base in a mountainous area.

Q256. *The Last of the Eastern Sea Forces Destroyed*

Assaut farouche en Cypre se prépare,
La larme à l'oeil, de ta tuine proche:

THE END OF THE WORLD

Byzance classe, Morisque si grande tare,
Deux différents, le grand vast par la roche.
  (XII,36,add.)

A ferocious attack will be made in Cyprus,
A tear drop in my eye, it will be you who will
  soon be ruined.
The Turkish and North African fleets will
  suffer great loss,
Both will drive themselves upon the rocks.

As a last effort to recover their losses in the
eastern Mediterranean, the Arabs will plan to use
Cyprus as a base of attack against Western advances
in southern Turkey and the Aegean. In a surprise
move, the Western forces will strike first, and ruin
Arab hopes of a victory and a turning of the tides
of battle. In the face of total destruction or immi-
nent capture, the last remaining Arab naval forces—
units from both Turkey and North Africa—will
scuttle themselves.

Q257. The Middle East Invaded

Nouvelle loi terre neuve occuper
Vers la Syrie, Iudée et Palestine:
Le grand empire, barbare corruer,
Avant que Phebes son siècle determine. (III,97)

A new force will occupy the new world,
The Allies will march against Syria, Judea
  and Palestine;
And the great Arab army will crumble,
All this will happen within a month's time.

From Turkey and Cyprus, Western forces will begin
infiltrating the heart of the Middle East, and stab
into occupied Israel, Lebanon, Syria and Jordan.
Arab resistance will begin to disintegrate under so
much pressure. Within a month from the day of
the attack on these countries, the last Eastern
forces [in Central and South America (Q188)]
will surrender, and Latin governments will be
re-established.

Q258–Q259. *Liberation of Israel*

Quand des croisés un trouvé de sens troublé,
En lieu du sacre verra un boeuf cornu:
Par vierge porc son lieu lors sera comblé,
Par Roi plus ordre ne sera soutenu. (VIII,90)

Et ne seront du tout leurs assaillements vains, et
au lieu que jadis fut l'habitation d'Abraham, sera
assaillie par personnes qui auront en vénération
les Jovialistes. Et icelle cité d'Achem sera en-
vironnée et assaillie de toutes parts en très-grande
puissance de gens d'armes. Seront affaibles leurs
forces maritimes par les Occidentaux. Et à ce
regne sera faite grande désolation, et les plus
grande cités seront dépeuplées et ceux qui entreront
dedans seront compris à la vengeance de l'ire de
Dieu. (Epistle to Henri II.)

When one of the crusaders will be found with
   his mind disturbed,
In the place of the holy one [Jersualem], one
   will see a horned ox [Taurus, i.e. the Arabs]:

The place of the virgin [Bethlehem] filled
with swine,
Order will not be maintained by the commander.

With attacks not in vain, the place where
Abraham lived [Israel], will be assaulted by
those who venerate the Jovialists [the Roman
Church]. The city of Achem [Schechem, north
Israel], will be surrounded and attacked on all
sides by the Westerners [European and Allies],
and great desolation will fall upon this realm.
Its greatest cities will be depopulated and
those who enter within will fall under the
vengeance of the wrath of God.

Israel will finally be invaded by the Allies, but at a
terrible price. The invasion will come from the
north, then drive southward toward Jerusalem and
Bethlehem, where sacred Christian shrines will be
found desecrated. Though freed from Arab control, Israel's major cities will for a long time be
uninhabitable because of something which may be
radiation poisoning or lingering chemical or bacteriological danger.

Q260. Preparation for an Attack on Iraq

La grande bande et secte crucigère
Se dressera en Mesopotamie:
Du proche fleuve campagnie légère,
Que telle loi tiendra pour ennemie. (III,61)

A large army of crusaders,
Will take up positions against Mesopotamia
  [Iraq],
A light company will defend a river,
And the enemy will hold his positions.

Having taken Israel and adjacent areas, the Western forces are now concentrating for an attack on Iraq, but the Arab forces will reorganize and offer them stiff resistance at a river.

Q261. The End of the Conflict Near

La foi Punicque en Orient rompue,
Gang. Iud, et Rosne, Loire, et Tag changeront:
Quand du mulet la faim sera repue,
Classe espargie, sang et corps nageront. (II,60)

The cold-hearted powers will be destroyed in
  the Orient,
The empire that included the Ganges [India],
  Jordan [Middle East], the Rhône and Loire
  [France], and Tagus [Spain] will be lost.
The hunger of the conqueror glutted,
Then the fleet will disperse him; blood and
  bodies will swim in the sea.

Toward the end of their existence as military powers unified by a common desire for world rule, the Easterners will be utterly annihilated in the Far East and the Middle Easterners will lose domination over Europe and even control over their own lands.

THE END OF THE WORLD
Q262. *Fighting in Southern Asia*

Un Duc cupide son ennemi ensuivre,
Dans entrera empêchant la phalange:
Hâtés à pied si près viendront poursuivre,
Que la journée conflict près de Gange. (IV,51)

A military leader will eagerly follow the retreat-
ing enemy,
He will penetrate their defenses and slow
their army:
They will be running on foot, and be pursued
very closely,
Finally they shall stop and fight near the
River Ganges.

The Westerners will open up a second front by
landing forces in south-west Asia and moving
against Middle Eastern positions in India. A Western commander will chase retreating Arab armies
and overtake them, forcing them to make a final
stand on the banks of the River Ganges.

Q263. *The Last Battles*

Aux champs de Mede, d'Arabe et d'Armenie,
Deux grandes copies trois fois s'assembleront:
Près du rivage d'Araxes la mesnie,
Du grand Soliman en terre tomberont. (III,31)

On two open plains of Media [east Iran],
Arabia and Armenia [south-west Russia],

221

The two sides will take up positions in all
    three areas.
A great number will assemble on the banks of
    the River Araxes, [south-west Russia],
There the great Suleiman [the Arabs] will fall
    to earth in defeat.

The last battles of the war will take place as the
Arabs make a last attempt to stop Western drives
into northern Arabia, eastern Iran and north-east
Turkey. The third battle will be the most important for it will bring the final collapse of the Arab
empire.

Q264. *Death of the Arab Commander-in-Chief*

Les deux malins de Scorpion conjoints,
Le grand Seigneur meurtri dans sa salle:
Peste à l'Église par le nouveau Roi joint,
L'Europe basse et Septentrionale. (I,52)

The two wicked ones [Mars and Saturn] in
    Scorpio,
The Sultan of the Middle East will die in the
    corridors of his command post.
The Church troubled by its new ally;
Europe still occupied from the north.

The military conflict will end with the death of
the commander-in-chief of all the Arab armies.
He will be killed in his own headquarters, and this
will signal the end of all organized Eastern resistance to the Western armies.

It appears, however, that the end of the war may not really be the end of the war after all. For the occupation of Europe by American and Russian forces is something that the Roman Catholic Church will have to deal with. Suddenly, the Pope will find himself at the whims, mercy and wishes of the occupying powers—and how long these powers will remain in control of demolished Europe is something Nostradamus does not even hint at.

Q265. World War III Ends in Iran

Pluie, fain, guerre en Perse non cessée,
La foi trop grande trahira le monarque,
Par la finie en Gaule commencée:
Secret augure pour à un être parque. (I, 70)

There will be rain and famine, fighting still
    going on in Iran,
The enemy leader will be betrayed by those
    of his own faith [Islam].
The war will end there that had begun in
    France:
A secret sign made not to be harsh.

In Europe the sound of cannon and rocketry, the blood of the wounded have been stopped, and the cries of the dying have been silenced, and the smoking ruins of the crumpled cities tell tales too horrible to be entrusted to words. Yet all is not over. The effects of radiation and bacterial contamination are still dangers the world has to contend with, as well as the cries of agony that hang over the conclusive battlefield of World War III somewhere in far-off Iran. Recognizing their final defeat, the last organized unit of the Arab army rebels against its commander, and forces him to surrender to the Western forces.

Tired of the bloodshed, and weary of the war, there will be no vengeance; only relief.

The War is at last ended.

Bibliography

Allen, Hugh; *Window in Provence*; Boston: Bruce Humphries, Inc, 1943.

Boswell, Rolfe; *Nostradamus Speaks*; New York: Thomas Y. Cromwell Co, 1941.

Brown, Florence V.; *Nostradamus: The Truth About Tomorrow*; New York: Tower Pb, Inc, 1970.

Carter, Mary Ellen; *Edgar Cayce on Prophecy*; New York: Paperback Library, Inc, 1968.

Criswell; *Criswell Predicts From Now to the Year 2000*; Anderson, S.C., Droke House, 1968.

Criswell; *Your Next Ten Years*; Anderson, S.C.; Droke House, 1969.

Forman, H.J.; *The Story of Prophecy*; New York: Tudor Publishing Co, 1940.

Glass, Justine; *They Foresaw the Future*; New York: G.P. Putnam's Sons, 1969.

Kahn, Herman and Weiner, Anthony J.; *The Year 2000*; New York: The Macmillan Company, 1967.

Lamont, Andri; *Nostradamus Sees All*; Philadelphia: W. Foulsham Co, 1944.

Laver, James; *Nostradamus*; London: Penguin Books, 1952.

Leoni, Edgar; *Nostradamus: Life and Literature*; New York: Exposition Press, 1961.

McCann, Lee, *Nostradamus: The Man Who Could See Through Time*; New York: Creative Age Press, 1941.

Montgomery, Ruth: *A Gift of Prophecy*; New York: Bantam Books, Inc, 1966.

Noorbergen, Rene; *Jeane Dixon: My Life and Prophecies*; New York: William Morrow & Co, 1970.

Robb, Stewart; *Nostradamus on Napoleon, Hitler and the Present Crisis*; New York: Charles Scribner's Sons, 1941.

Robb, Stewart; *Prophecies on World Events by Nostradamus*; New York: Liveright Publishing Corp, 1961.

Robb, Stewart; *Strange Prophecies That Came True*; New York: Ace Books, Inc, 1967.

Roberts, Henry C.; *The Complete Prophecies of Nostradamus*; New York: Nostradamus, Inc, 1949.

Timbs, John; *Predictions Realized in Modern Times*; London: Lockwood and Co, 1880.

Ward, Charles A.; *Oracles of Nostradamus*; New York: Charles Scribner's Sons, 1940.